Sweet

Surprises

presented by

California Home Economics Teachers

Editor: Gerry Henderson

Graphics: Laura Pierce

© California Management Services MCMLXXXIV
116 S. Waterwheel Way, Orange, California 92669

© Library of Congress Catalog
Card No. 83-072739
ISBN 0-914159-00-3

SWEET SURPRISES

When I was a little boy in Stamford, Texas, coming back to the farm house after completing the chores, my favorite question was, "What's for dessert, Mom?" (Never mind the meal . . . just what's the *SWEET SURPRISE!*) Everybody loves desserts and *SWEET SURPRISES* offers you the finest collection of dessert recipes that California Home Economics Teachers can compile. Many are family favorites, and yes, I had to include my favorite from my mother! (Page 74)

Who are the "professional home economists" who wrote these recipes? They are first and foremost educators, who understand the culinary arts and how to teach those skills to students. Therefore, you will find these dessert recipes and instructions simple, direct and delicious!

To all these recipe contributors whose names and schools are listed beneath their recipes, we owe a sincere word of thanks. To the staff of California Mananagement Services who devoted many hours towards collecting these recipes . . . thanks, guys, you're fun to work with! (Howard Bronson, Russ Herrema, Steve Baker, Doug Herrema, Doug Pierce, and Lynda McGrath). To Laura Pierce, the designer, we are grateful for her creative artwork. For Phil and Norma Elkins, my faithful partners in California Management Services, there could never be too many "thank you's".

Thanks also to Baskin Robbins, Hersheys, and Pillsbury, for all the color photography which you'll find within. We hope that you as the purchaser are pleased with the book.

And to one fine lady in particular, Gerry Murray Henderson (and her husband, Jim), formerly of Glendora High School and now of Temple City High, the Editor of *SWEET SURPRISES* (as well as other books we have done in the past), I say, "Thank you, Gerry, I could not have published this book without you."

Sincerely,
Grady W. Reed
President
California Management Services
Cookbook Division

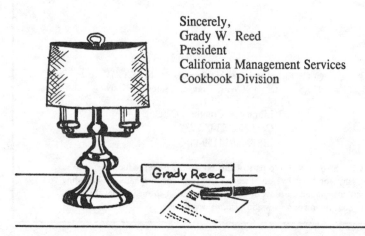

CALIFORNIA HOME ECONOMICS TEACHERS ADVISORY COMMITTEE

Anderson, Jill
Santa Paula HS, Santa Paula

Black-Eacker, Ellen
Nogales HS, La Puente

Cain, Joy Nell
Willowood JHS, West Covina

Dempsy, Jean
Santa Paula HS, Santa Paula

Fosdick, Karen
Cajon HS, San Bernardino

Frank, Polly
Lakewood HS, Lakewood

Friederichsen, Jan
Vista Del Rio JHS, Orange

Glennan, Renee
Sequoia JHS, Simi Valley

Gremmel, Judy
Westminster HS, Westminster

Henderson, Gerry
Temple City HS, Temple City

Hibma, Grace
Office of Los Angeles County
Superintendent of Schools, Consultant,
Consumer & Homemaking Education

Himenes, Peggy
Actis JHS, Bakersfield

Hulen, Cheryl
Hemet HS, Hemet

Hulen, Donna
Los Alamitos HS, Los Alamitos

Huntzinger, Susan
Glendale HS, Glendale

Lash, Mary
Paramount HS, Paramount

Lentz, Jeri
Grossmont HS, Grossmont

Lopez, Karen
San Luis Obispo HS, San Luis Obispo

Marcus, Meridith
San Pasqual HS, Escondido

Matsuno, Dale
Montebello Intermediate School,
Montebello

Mitchell, Eudora
Norwalk HS, Norwalk

Muraoka, June
Cypress HS, Cypress

Nelson, Peggy
Norte Vista HS, Riverside

Pace, Sally
Woodlake HS, Woodlake

Pendleton, Susie
Cerritos HS, Cerritos

Phipps, Louise
Washington Middle School, Vista

Pereira, Marilyn
Hanford HS, Hanford

Priestley, Roberta
Alhambra HS, Alhambra

Pringle, Adrienne
Valley View JHS, Simi Valley

Rayl, Charla
El Toro HS, El Toro

Reser, Ione
Hesperia JHS, Hesperia

Reza, Maria
Supervisor, Home Economics
Los Angeles Unified School District

Richmond, Mary E.
San Luis Obispo HS, San Luis Obispo

Rupp, Janet
Vista Del Rio JHS, Orange

Tadros, Elaine
Palm Desert Middle School, Palm Desert

Traw, Marianne
Ball JHS, Anaheim

Warren, Kit
Edison HS, Huntington Beach

West, Ruby
Elliott JHS, Pasadena

Wildermuth, Ellie
La Canada HS, La Canada

Wong, Pat
Taft HS, Taft

Wolfe, Margaret
Woodlake HS, Woodlake

COLOR PHOTOGRAPHY CREDITS

Cover Photograph: Courtesy of Baskin-Robbins Ice Cream of Glendale, California

Interior Photographs: Courtesy of Hershey Foods Corporation of Hershey, Pennsylvania

Courtesy of The Pillsbury Company of Minneapolis, Minnesota

COLOR PHOTOGRAPHED RECIPES

Mini Chip Brownies, page 42
Choco-Bar Fondue, page 72
Coconut Surprise, page 58
Jamoca Volcano, page 58
Ice Cream Sopaipillas, page 59
Cool Chocolate Souffle, page 114
Cool Chocolate Cream Pie, page 99
Heavenly Heart Chocolate Cake, page 2
Macaroon Kiss Cookies, page 45
Pears Au Chocolat, page 73
Old-Fashioned Chocolate Ice Cream, page 66
Marble Chiffon Cake, page 16
Fudge Chiffon Pie, page 106
Pina Colada Party Cake, page 15

TO ORDER ADDITIONAL COPIES OF SWEET SURPRISES

Send name, address, and $7.30 (includes tax and postage) to:

California Management Services
116 So. Waterwheel Way
Orange, California 92669

Other books available at $7.30 (includes tax and postage) are:

International Cuisine
A Matter of Taste

Those available at $6.25 (includes tax and postage) are:

Fiesta Favorites
Light Cuisine
Simple Selections

Contents

On our cover:

a. Jamoca Volcano, 58
b. Coconut Surprise, 58
c. Sopaipillas, 59

Courtesy of Baskin Robbins Ice Cream®

Prize winning recipes; 1981 Ice Cream Show-off Recipe Contest

Notes

Cakes &
Frostings

Heavenly Heart Chocolate Cake

¾ cup unsweetened cocoa
⅔ cup boiling water
¾ cup butter or margarine, softened
2 cups sugar
1 teaspoon vanilla
2 eggs

2 cups unsifted cake flour or 1-¾ cups all-
    purpose flour
1 ¼ teaspoons baking soda
¼ teaspoon salt
¾ cup buttermilk or sour milk*

Stir together cocoa and boiling water in small bowl until smooth; set aside. Cream butter or margarine, sugar and vanilla in large mixer bowl until fluffy; beat in eggs and cocoa mixture. Combine flour, baking soda, and salt; add alternately with buttermilk or sour milk to creamed mixture. Pour batter into two greased and floured heart-shaped pans or two 9-inch layer pans. Bake at 350° for 30 to 35 minutes or until cake tester inserted in center comes out clean. Cool 10 minutes; remove from pans. Cool completely; frost with Glossy Chocolate Sour Cream Frosting and pipe with Creamy Butter Cream Frosting. Sprinkle with chopped nuts, if desired.

*To sour milk: Use 2 teaspoons vinegar plus milk to equal ¾ cup.

Glossy Chocolate Sour Cream Frosting

1 ½ cups semi-sweet chocolate Mini Chips
¾ cup sour cream

2 cups confectioner's sugar
1 teaspoon vanilla

Melt Mini Chips in top of double boiler over hot water. Stir constantly until completely melted. Remove from heat; beat in sour cream, confectioners' sugar and vanilla. About 2 ½ cups frosting.

Creamy Buttercream Frosting

2 cups confectioner's sugar
¼ cup butter or margarine

2 ½ tablespoons milk
½ teaspoon vanilla

Combine ingredients until smooth and creamy in a small bowl. With decorating tube, pipe frosting around edges of cake. About 1 cup frosting.
Hershey Foods Corporation   **Hershey, Pennsylvania**

Chocolate Cake

2 oz. chocolate, grated
1 cup boiling water
½ cup shortening
2 cups sugar
½ teaspoon salt

2 cups flour
1 ½ teaspoons baking soda
½ cup sour milk
2 eggs, beaten

Heat chocolate, water and shortening until melted and mixture is glossy when beaten slightly. Remove from heat and place mixture in a bowl. Add remaining ingredients in order listed. Beat vigorously 2 minutes. (Batter will be very thin). Do not add more flour. Pour batter into two greased 8" cake pans. Bake at 350°F for 30-35 minutes.
Joanne Sands   **Morse High School, San Diego**

Recipe for "Heavenly Heart Chocolate Cake" on page 2 →
Recipe for "Macaroon Kiss Cookies" on page 45 →

Black Forest Cake

1 Pillsbury German Chocolate cake mix	3 eggs
1/3 cup Hershey cocoa	1 can Wilderness cherry pie filling
1 cup water	1/2 pint whipping cream
1/3 cup oil	1/2 can Pillsbury chocolate fudge frosting

Add cake mix, cocoa, water, oil and eggs to electric mixer bowl. Beat at low speed to mix. Beat 2 minutes at higher speed. Pour into two greased 9" cake pans. Bake at 350°F for 25-35 minutes. Cool in pans 15 minutes. Remove from pans and cool. Wrap loosely in Saran Wrap and refrigerate overnight. Unwrap and put cake layer on flat plate. Put about half of cherry filling on layer leaving 1 inch outer edge without filling. Place second layer on top of filling. Frost sides of cake with chocolate frosting. Whip cream. With teaspoon, put whipped cream in mounds around other edge of cake. Pour remaining cherry pie filling in center. Refrigerate. Serves 12.

"Freezes well. Microwave o.k. Not necessary to include brand names in recipe. Use any chocolate cake mix, but I prefer this one. Do not use Dream Whip or Cool Whip. Must be whipping cream."

Pauline S. Jones (Retired)   *Cabrillo Junior High School, Ventura*

Aunt Jayne's Twenty-Minute Chocolate Cake

2 cups sugar	3 tablespoons cocoa
2 cups sifted flour	2 beaten eggs
1/2 teaspoon salt	1/2 cup sour milk or 1/2 cup milk plus 1
1 teaspoon baking soda	tablespoon vinegar)
2 sticks margarine (1 cup)	1 teaspoon vanilla
1 cup water	

*Frosting: recipe below

In a large bowl mix sugar, flour, salt and soda; set aside. In a saucepan, bring to a boil the margarine, water, and cocoa. Add to dry ingredients in bowl. Add eggs, sour milk and vanilla. Mix. Pour batter into a (10½ x 15½" Jelly Roll Pan), and bake at 350°F for 20 minutes. Frost the cake in the pan as soon as it comes out of the oven.

*Frosting:	
1/2 cup margarine or butter	6 tablespoons milk
3 tablespoons cocoa	1 box powdered sugar (sifted)
	1 teaspoon vanilla

Mix all ingredients together with an electric mixer. Spread over warm cake. Cool and cut.

"Be sure to use the right size pan. This recipe was given to me by my Aunt Jayne. We bake it for everyone's Birthday cake."

Marianne Traw   *Ball Jr High School, Anaheim*

← Recipe for "Pina Colada Party Cake" on page 15

Hit and Miss Cake & Broiled Coconut Frosting

1 ½ cups flour
1 teaspoon baking soda
¼ teaspoon salt
5 tablespoons + 1 teaspoon cocoa
1 cup sugar

1 teaspoon vinegar
½ teaspoon vanilla
6 tablespoons salad oil
1 cup warm water

Broiled Coconut Frosting:
¼ cup margarine or butter
¾ cup brown sugar

2-3 tablespoons canned milk
¾ cup coconut
few drops vanilla

Put all dry ingredients into an 8 x 8″ pan *which has been well greased*. Make 3 *well* holes in mixture with spoon. In 1 hole put vinegar, in 1 hole put vanilla, and in 1 hole put oil. Pour 1 cup warm water over entire mixture and blend gently but thoroughly with fork. *Do Not Beat!!!* Bake at 350°F for 25-30 minutes. Frost with Broiled Coconut Frosting while warm.

Frosting: Cream butter and sugar. Add milk, mix well. Stir in coconut and vanilla. Spread over *warm* cake. Broil 2-3 minutes until golden brown or bubbly. Serve warm. Serves 6-9.

Mildred Walls   *El Dorado High School, Placentia*

Kentucky Cream Cake and Frosting

½ cup vegetable shortening
1 stick margarine (½ cup)
2 cups sugar
5 egg yolks
2 ¼ cups all-purpose flour
1 teaspoon baking soda

1 cup buttermilk
1 teaspoon vanilla
1 cup coconut
⅔ cup chopped walnuts
5 egg whites, beaten

Frosting:

1 (8 oz.) cream cheese
½ stick margarine (¼ cup)
1 teaspoon vanilla

1 pound box powdered sugar
½ cup chopped nuts

Cream shortening and margarine with sugar. Add egg yolks, one at a time. Beat well. Add flour and baking soda alternately with buttermilk and vanilla, coconut and nuts; fold in beaten egg whites. Bake in two or three 8 x 8 x 2″ layers at 350°F for 35 to 40 minutes

Frosting: Cream first four ingredients together. Frost cake. Put chopped nuts on top of cake.

Lillian Lee   *Hanford High School, Hanford*

Poppyseed Cake

Cake:
3/4 cup butter or margarine
1 1/2 cups sugar
1/4 teaspoon salt
1/3 cup poppyseed
1 cup milk

2 1/4 cups flour, sifted
2 1/2 teaspoons baking powder
4 egg whites
1 teaspoon vanilla

Filling:
1/2 cup sugar
1/8 teaspoon salt
3 tablespoons cornstarch
2 cups milk
4 egg yolks, beaten
1 tablespoon butter
1 teaspoon vanilla
1 cup pecans, chopped

Frosting:
2 squares unsweetened chocolate
1/4 cup butter
1/4 cup cold milk
1 cup powdered sugar
1 large egg
1 teaspoon vanilla

Cream butter, sugar and salt. Soak poppyseed in water for 2 hours or overnight. Drain poppyseed and add to creamed mixture. Add milk alternately with sifted flour and baking powder. Fold in stiffly beaten egg whites and vanilla. Bake in three 8" layer pans which are well buttered. (I put brown paper on the bottoms). Bake at 350°F for 20-25 minutes. Cool. Spread filling between layers and frost.

Filling: Mix sugar, salt and cornstarch in saucepan. Add milk and cook over low heat for 10 minutes. Add some of the hot mixture to egg yolks, then return to pan and cook until thick. Remove from heat. Add butter, vanilla and nuts. Cool. Spread between cake layers.

Frosting: Melt chocolate and butter in a double boiler over very low heat. Set in *cold* water, add remaining ingredients, and beat with electric mixer until stiff. Frost cake.
Phyllis Kaylor   *Einstein Junior High School, San Diego*

Top of the Mark Tweed Cake

Cake:
1/2 cup (1 cube butter)
1/2 cup sugar
2 cups cake flour
3 teaspoons baking powder
pinch of salt
1 cup milk

2 teaspoons vanilla
3 squares (1 oz. each) unsweetened baking
   chocolate
3 egg whites
1/2 cup sugar

Frosting:
1/2 cup (1 cube) soft butter
3 egg yolks
2 cups sifted powdered sugar
2 teaspoons vanilla

Chocolate Glaze:
1/2 pkg. (6 oz.) semi-sweet chocolate chips
2 tablespoons water

5

Cream together thoroughly butter and sugar. Sift flour, measure and sift with the baking powder and salt. Add dry ingredients to creamed mixture alternately with milk combined with vanilla, beginning and ending with dry ingredients. After each addition beat until smooth. Coarsely grate chocolate. Blend into batter. Beat egg whites until foamy and add the ½ cup sugar a tablespoon at a time; beat until stiff. Carefully fold into batter. Pour into three 8" round layer cake pans or two 9" pans, greased and floured. Bake in a moderate oven 325° for 20-25 minutes or until toothpick inserted in center comes out clean. Cool slightly. Turn layers out of pans; cool thoroughly on wire racks. Frost between layers and top and sides. Drizzle glaze over top of cake, allowing to drop down sides.

Frosting: Beat together butter and egg yolks. Blend powdered sugar into butter and egg mixture until smooth. Frost cake.

Chocolate Glaze: Melt chocolate chips in top part of a double boiler. Add water and stir until smooth. Drizzle over cake as directed. (This glaze could be done in the microwave). Serves 12.

"Won 1st Prize at a County Fair!"
Pat Storms   *Anna McKenney Intermediate School, Marysville*

Raisin Cake

3 cups unsifted flour
2 cups sugar
1 cup mayonnaise
⅓ cup milk
2 eggs
2 teaspoons baking soda
1 ½ teaspoons cinnamon

½ teaspoon nutmeg
⅓ teaspoon salt
¼ teaspoon ground cloves
3 cups apples
1 cup raisins
½ cup walnuts
2 cups whipped cream

Grease and flour two 9" pans. Mix first 10 ingredients together for two minutes. Stir in apples, raisins and nuts. Bake at 350° for 45 minutes. Fill and frost with two cups whipped cream.

Linda Boyd   *Claremont High School, Claremont*

Busy Day Cake

1 ⅔ cups flour
¼ teaspoon salt
1 cup sugar
2 ½ teaspoons baking powder

⅓ cup shortening
1 teaspoon vanilla
1 egg (unbeaten)
⅔ cup milk (room temperature)

Topping:
3 tablespoons melted butter
4 tablespoons brown sugar

2 tablespoons evaporated milk
½ cup coconut (shredded or flaked)

Preheat oven to 350°F. Grease an 8" square pan or an 8 ½ or 9" inch round cake pan. Sift flour, salt, sugar and baking powder. Add shortening, vanilla, egg (unbeaten) and milk

all together. Beat well with rotary beater for two minutes. Pour into prepared pan. Bake for 25-35 minutes at 350°F.

While cake is baking prepare topping: combine all four ingredients for topping in a small bowl. Spread on top of cake after it comes out of oven while it is still warm. Put under broiler for a minute or so; watch carefully. Serves 6.

"Very economical and simple to make. Extremely moist and tasty. Originally from newspaper or magazine during the Second World War."
Constance M. Battu   *Meller Junior High School, Pico Rivera*

Carrot Cake with Cream Cheese Frosting

1-½ cups vegetable oil	*2 teaspoons baking powder*
1 cup white sugar	*2 teaspoons cinnamon*
½ cup brown sugar	*1 teaspoon salt*
4 eggs	*3 cups finely shredded carrots*
2 cups flour	*1 cup chopped nuts, optional*
2 teaspoons baking soda	

Frosting:	*2 teaspoons vanilla*
1 (3 oz.) package cream cheese	*½ box powdered sugar*
½ stick margarine	

Combine oil and sugars, beating until well blended. Add eggs, one at a time, mixing well. Sift dry ingredients together and add to batter gradually. Beat until smooth. Add carrots and nuts. Beat ½ minute. Pour into a 13 x 9″ pan. Bake 45 minutes at 300°F or until toothpick comes out clean. Cool.

Frosting: Cream butter and cream cheese together; add vanilla and sugar, gradually. Beat until smooth. Frost cake. Serves 10-12.

"Refrigerate to store."
Marge Dieterich   *West Covina High School, West Covina*

Mom's Raw Apple Cake

1 cup sugar	*½ cup warm coffee (liquid)*
½ cup shortening	*2 cups raw apples*
1 egg	
1 ½ cup flour	**Topping:**
1 teaspoon cinnamon	*½ cup brown sugar*
1 teaspoon soda	*½ teaspoon cinnamon*
½ teaspoon nutmeg	*½ cup nuts*

Mix ingredients in the order given. Pour in an oblong baking dish or pan (13 x 9″). Sprinkle with topping, (½ cup brown sugar, ½ teaspoon cinnamon and ½ cup nuts mixed together). Bake in 350°F oven for 35 minutes. Serve with whipped cream or Cool Whip. Serves 10-12.

R.P. Alston   *Hosler Junior High School, Lynwood*

Blackberry Jam Cake

2 cups flour
1 teaspoon soda
½ teaspoon cinnamon
½ teaspoon allspice
½ teaspoon nutmeg
½ cup shortening or margarine
1 cup jam

1 cup brown sugar
1 teaspoon vanilla
1 cup sour milk or buttermilk
¾ cup chopped nuts
Cream cheese frosting or powdered sugar
(optional)

Grease and flour a 9 x 12" cake pan. Sift together flour, soda, cinnamon, allspice and nutmeg. Cream shortening and jam together. Add brown sugar and vanilla. Add alternating milk and dry ingredients. Fold in nuts. Bake in 350°F oven 30-40 minutes. May be frosted with cream cheese frosting or dusted with powdered sugar. Serves 10-12.

"This cake has been handed down for generations in my family. Rich and should be moist."
Nancy Voyles   **Canyon High School, Anaheim**

Applesauce Cake

½ cup margarine
1 cup brown sugar
1 cup white sugar
1 egg
2 cups applesauce
2 teaspoons baking soda
2 ½ cups flour

2 teaspoons cinnamon
1 teaspoon cloves
½ teaspoon nutmeg
2 tablespoons unsweetened cocoa
1 teaspoon salt
1 cup nuts
1 cup raisins (optional)

Cream together margarine, brown sugar, white sugar and egg. In a small bowl, combine applesauce and baking soda; then add to sugar mixture. Sift together flour, cinnamon, cloves, nutmeg, cocoa and salt. Add to sugar mixture. Stir in nuts and raisins (optional).

Bake in a greased 9 x 13" pan or two 8" round pans for 25-30 minutes at 350°F. Frost with chocolate frosting, if desired. Serves 15.
Cathy Smith   **Lone Hill Intermediate School, San Dimas**

Chocolate Chip Date Cake

1 cup chopped dates
1 cup hot water
1 teaspoon soda
1 cup sugar
1 cup shortening
2 eggs

¼ teaspoon salt
1 tablespoon cocoa
1 ¾ cups sifted flour
1 6-oz. pkg. chocolate chips
½ cup walnuts, chopped

Combine the dates, water and soda and let stand. Cream the sugar and shortening and then add the eggs, salt, cocoa and flour. Add the date mixture alternately with the dry

ingredients. Add ½ package of the chocolate chips to the mixture and pour into a greased and floured 9 x 13" pan. Sprinkle with the remaining chocolate chips and the chopped walnuts. Bake at 350°F for 40-50 minutes. Serves 12.

"Good, easy, no messy frosting, stays moist."
Merideth Marcus   **San Pasqual High School, Escondido**

Self-Frosting Date Cake

1 cup pitted dates
1 ¼ cup hot water
1 teaspoon baking soda
1 ¾ cup sifted flour
1 teaspoon baking powder
1 teaspoon salt
¾ cup shortening

1 cup sugar
2 eggs

Topping:
1 6-oz. pkg of semi-sweet chocolate pieces
¾ cup firmly packed brown sugar
½ cup chopped nuts

Grease and lightly flour a 9 x 13" cake pan; preheat oven to 350°F. Cut dates into fine pieces. Add hot water and soda. Let stand until cool. Sift together flour, baking powder, salt, and set aside. Cream shortening and sugar together well. Add eggs and beat well. Add cooled date mixture. Beat well. Stir in the dry ingredients gradually, mixing well after each addition. Pour into the greased and floured cake pan. Add the topping *before* baking: Combine topping ingredients and sprinkle evenly over cake. Bake 40-50 minutes. Serve warm or cold. Serves 18.

Mary Kantola   **Matthew Gage Middle School, Riverside**

Sin on a Plate (Triple Chocolate Cake)

1 18½-oz. box deep chocolate or
  devil's food cake mix
1 4-oz. box instant chocolate pudding
¾ cup sour cream
½ cup vegetable oil
½ cup water
½ cup toasted chopped almonds
¼ cup mayonnaise
4 eggs

3 tablespoons almond liqueur (Amaretto)
1 teaspoon almond extract
1 cup chocolate chips

Glaze:
1 cup powdered sugar
3 tablespoons milk
1 teaspoon almond extract

Preheat oven to 350°F. Grease a 10" bundt pan and dust with cocoa. Place all ingredients except chocolate chips in a large bowl and beat 2 minutes with electric mixer on medium speed. Mix in chocolate chips. Pour into prepared pan. Bake 50-55 minutes or until cake tests done. Cool on rack 10 minutes before removing from pan. Place warm cake on serving dish and drizzle with glaze.

Glaze: Mix all ingredients thoroughly in small bowl. Let stand at room temperature until ready to glaze. Serves 10-12.

Carleen Street   **Wasco Union High School, Wasco**

Banana Split Cake

1 cup graham cracker crumbs
¼ cup melted butter or margarine
2 cups powdered sugar
½ cup butter or margarine
1 egg

3 bananas, sliced
1 8-oz. can crushed pineapple, drained
½ 9-oz. carton of Cool Whip
½ cup chopped nuts
5 maraschino cherries, halved

Mix graham cracker crumbs and ¼ cup butter or margarine together and press into the bottom of an 8 x 8 x 2" square baking pan. Beat together powdered sugar, ½ cup butter or margarine and egg until smooth, (about 10 minutes). Spread powdered sugar mixture on top of crust. Place sliced bananas and crushed pineapple on top of powdered sugar mixture. Spread Cool Whip on top of bananas and pineapple, and garnish with chopped nuts and maraschino cherries. Refrigerate several hours or overnight. Serves 4-6.

Sandy Mori   *Alhambra High School, Alhambra*

Mississippi Mud Cake

4 eggs
2 cups sugar
2 cubes melted butter
1 ½ cup flour
⅓ cup cocoa
1 teaspoon vanilla
1 cup coconut
1-2 cups nuts
1 7-oz. jar marshmallow creme

Frosting:
1 cube melted butter
6 tablespoons milk
⅓ cup cocoa
1 lb. powdered sugar (sifted)
1 teaspoon vanilla
1 cup nuts

Combine eggs and sugar, beat until thick. Combine melted butter, flour, cocoa, vanilla, coconut and nuts and add to eggs and sugar. Pour into a greased and floured 9 x 13" pan. Bake about 30-40 minutes at 350°F. When just out of the oven, spread marshmallow creme on top. Let cool, then frost. To make frosting: melt butter, add milk, cocoa, powdered sugar and vanilla and beat well. Add nuts.

Shirley Marshman   *West Middle School, Downey*

Brownie Pudding Cake

2 cups flour
1 ½ cups sugar
¼ cup cocoa
4 teaspoons baking powder
1 teaspoon salt
1 cup milk

¼ cup salad oil
2 teaspoons vanilla
1 ½ cups chopped nuts
1 ½ cups brown sugar
½ cup cocoa

Sift together the first five ingredients. Add milk, salad oil and vanilla. Stir in nuts. Pour into a greased 9 x 13" pan. Mix together 1-½ cups brown sugar and ½ cup cocoa. Sprinkle over the batter. Pour 3-½ cups hot water over entire batter. Bake at 350°F for 45 minutes.

Cari Maze   *Dexter Intermediate School, Whittier*

10

Pumpkin Pie Cake

2 eggs
1 can pumpkin (1 lb.)
¾ cup sugar
½ teaspoon salt
1 teaspoon cinnamon
½ teaspoon ginger

¼ teaspoon cloves
1 ⅔ cups evaporated milk
Whipped cream for topping
1 cube margarine
1 box spice cake mix

Beat eggs slightly with an electric mixer; add pumpkin, sugar, spices and milk. Mix until well blended. Pour into a greased 9 x 12 cake pan. Sprinkle dry cake mix over pumpkin mixture. Melt margarine and drizzle over cake mix. Bake in a 350°F oven for 30-40 minutes. Cut into squares and serve with a dollop of whipped cream on top. Serves 15-20.

"Easy to make and take to fall pot-luck dinners."
Marianne Estes   *La Mirada High School, La Mirada*

Delicious Layered Cake

1 yellow cake mix
1 3-oz. cream cheese
2 tablespoons milk
1 pkg. instant lemon pudding

1 can crushed pineapple, drained
1 9-oz. Cool Whip Topping
½ cup slivered almonds
¼ cup maraschino cherries, drained

Make cake mix according to the directions on the package. Bake the cake in a 9 x 13" greased and floured pan for 20 minutes at 350°F. Cool the cake. Soften the cream cheese with 2 tablespoons of milk and spread on the cake. Mix the lemon instant pudding according to the package directions. Pour the lemon pudding on top of the cake. Refrigerate for one hour. Pour the drained pineapple on the top. Top with the Cool Whip, slivered almonds and cherries. Refrigerate. Serves 10-15.

"This delicious cake will stay fresh for one week."
Bonnie Landin   *Garden Grove High School, Garden Grove*

Cherry Yummy

3-4 cans cherry pie filling
1 pkg. white cake mix
2 cubes butter, melted

1 cup walnuts (chopped)
ice cream, vanilla

Empty cherries into an 11 x 15" baking dish. Sprinkle dry cake mix evenly over top of cherries. Pour butter over cake mix. Sprinkle walnuts on top. Bake at 350°F for one hour. Cool 30 minutes. Spoon ice cream on top. Serves 12.

'Can be frozen and re-heated."
Rita Kramer   *Montebello High School, Montebello*

Fruit Cocktail Cake

1 cup enriched flour
¼ cup sugar
1 ½ teaspoons baking powder
½ teaspoon salt
1 egg
¼ cup fruit cocktail syrup
¼ cup packed dark brown sugar

½ teaspoon vanilla extract
½ can (15 oz.) fruit cocktail,
    drained (about ½ cup)
½ cup chopped nuts
3 ½ teaspoons packed dark brown sugar
Whipped cream or ice cream for topping

Preheat oven to 325°F. Grease a 9 x 9" pan. Stir together flour, sugar, baking powder and salt. In a separate bowl, beat together egg, fruit cocktail syrup, ¼ cup brown sugar and vanilla. Add liquid to flour mixture; mix well. Fold in drained fruit and nuts. Pour batter into greased pan. Sprinkle brown sugar over cake batter. Bake in preheated oven for 45 minutes. Serve with whipped cream or ice cream. Make one 9 x 9" pan.

Donna Swennes   **El Capitan High School, Lakeside**

Turtle Cake

1 box German Chocolate cake mix
1 14-oz. bag caramels
½ cup evaporated milk

¾ cup butter
2 cups chopped walnuts
1 cup miniature chocolate chips

Prepare cake mix using package directions. Pour half of the batter into a greased 9 x 14" baking dish. Bake at 350°F for 20 minutes. Melt caramels with evaporated milk and butter in a saucepan over low heat, stirring constantly. Pour over cake. Sprinkle with 1 cup nuts and 1 cup chocolate chips. Pour remaining batter over filling. Sprinkle with remaining 1 cup walnuts. Bake for 25-30 minutes. Serves 18.

Betty Ferber   **Rowland High School, Rowland Heights**

Cake with Strawberries

1 box strawberry Jello (small)
1 cup hot water
1 box frozen strawberries
1 large pkg. Philadelphia cream cheese

1 cup sugar
1 package Dream Whip
1 large baked white cake

Mix Jello with 1 cup of hot water, then add the strawberries. Let mixture set a little. Combine cheese and sugar, beat well then add *one* package Dream Whip that has been beaten thoroughly. Stir together with Jello mixture. Bake one large white cake and break into pieces. Put the pieces in a large, (13-½ x 8-¾"), pan and pour the above mixture over it. I usually use a fork and poke here and there, to let the cream mixture through. Put in the refrigerator overnight or several hours before serving.

"If you freeze your own strawberries with sugar, (for syrup), the pint size is fine. While the cake is baking, you should have ample time for preparing other ingredients."

Virginia Young   **Washington Junior High School, Dinuba**

Strawberry Angel Food

1 pkg. frozen strawberries
1 small Angel food cake

½ pint whipping cream
1 envelope gelatin

Thaw strawberries in medium mixing bowl until separated and are juicy, but still cold. Break cake into pieces and put into an 8 x 10″ pan or dish. Whip cream and set aside. Soften gelatin in ¼ cup cold water, adding ½ cut hot water to dissolve. Pour into bowl with strawberries and juice, mixing well. It should begin to thicken if cold enough. Fold in whipped cream and pour over cake. Coat with a fork to get in between the pieces. Place in refrigerator for 2 hours or more. Serves 10.

"Don't worry about leftovers, there won't be any!"

Imogene Wicker   **Granada Intermediate School, Whittier**

Cherry Angel Cake

1 large Angel food cake
2 cans cherry pie filling
1 3-oz. pkg. instant vanilla pudding

1 ½ cups milk
½ pint sour cream

In a 9 x 13″ pan (or any convenient size) break half of the Angel food cake into pieces and place in pan. Cover with 1 can cherry pie filling. Add other half of cake (layer on cherries). Mix pudding, milk, sour cream and beat until the mixture is smooth. Pour over layers in pan. Top with remaining can of cherry pie filling and refrigerate. Serve by spooning into dish or on saucer or plate. Serves 12+ .

"This is a favorite dessert at 'the beginning of school luncheon' put on by the parents for the teachers."

Willy Hall   **McPherson Jr. High School, Orange**

Flower Garden Cake

¾ cup sugar
¾ cup fruit juice (2 lemons,
    rest orange or pineapple juice)
6 egg yolks
1 envelope Knox gelatin dissolved
    in ¼ cup water

6 beaten egg whites
¾ cup sugar
1 Angel food cake

Make a custard of ¾ cup sugar, fruit juice and egg yolks. Cook until mixture coats the spoon. Remove from heat and add gelatin dissolved in cold water; cool. Beat egg whites, add sugar gradually, beating until they hold peaks. Fold egg whites into cooked custard. Grease pan with butter. Break cake into bite-size pieces. Place in pan in alternate layers starting with cake, then custard. Cover with waxed paper. Let stand in refrigerator overnight.

Jean Jeter   **Park View Intermediate School, Lancaster**

Grandma's Strawberry Cake

1 pkg. white cake mix
3 tablespoons flour
1 3-oz. pkg. strawberry Jello
4 eggs
1 cup Crisco or Wesson Oil
½ pkg. strawberries
    (10 oz. frozen or fresh)
½ cup water

Icing:
½ cube butter
½ pkg. strawberries
    (10 oz. frozen or fresh)
1 box powdered sugar

Mix all ingredients together and blend well (except icing). Pour into greased and floured 13 x 9" cake pan. Bake at 350°F according to time on box of cake mix. Ice when cool.

Icing: Mix ingredients together and use to frost strawberry cake. Serves 10.

Karen Lopez   *San Luis Obispo Senior High School, San Luis Obispo*

Pina Colada Cake

8-oz. can crushed pineapple, packed
    in its own juice
½ cup flaked coconut
18 ½-oz. box pineapple flavored cake mix
    (not pudding-added type)
4 ¾-oz. box instant vanilla pudding
4 eggs
½ cup cooking oil
½ cup dark rum
½ cup cream of coconut
coconut (for garnish)

Rum Sauce:
¼ pound butter
⅓ cup sugar
3 tablespoons pineapple juice
    (reserved from cake)
3 tablespoons rum (dark)
4 tablespoons cream of coconut

Drain pineapple, reserving juice. Mix pineapple with flaked coconut and set aside. Grease and flour a 12-cup bundt pan and preheat oven to 350°F. Combine cake mix, pudding, eggs, oil, rum and cream of coconut in a large mixing bowl and beat for 2 minutes with electric mixer at high speed. Fold in pineapple/coconut mixture. Pour into prepared pan and bake for 1 ½ to 1 ¾ hours, checking occasionally from the hour mark on. Cake is done when it is nicely browned and a testing pick comes out clean. While cake bakes, prepare Rum Sauce:

In a small saucepan, combine butter, sugar and pineapple juice. Heat over low flame until butter melts and sugar dissolves. Bring to boil and boil one minute. Remove from heat and let cool about 10 minutes. Stir in rum and cream of coconut.

When cake is done, remove from oven, let cool only a short time, and punch holes in surface with fork or testing pick. Drizzle half of rum sauce over cake. Let cake cool in pan another 15 minutes. Turn out on serving plate. Punch holes in top and upper sides and spoon remaining sauce over cake. Garnish with extra flaked coconut if you wish. Let cool completely before cutting.

Jackie Wisherd   *Woodrow Wilson Junior High School, San Diego*

Pina Colada Party Cake

1 cup coconut
1 pkg. Pillsbury Plus White Cake Mix
½ cup water
½ cup pineapple juice
⅓ cup oil
¼ cup rum*
4 egg whites
½ cup pineapple juice
½ cup sugar

Frosting:
1 can Pillsbury Ready to Spread Vanilla
   Frosting Supreme
1 tablespoon rum or ½ teaspoon rum extract
½ cup reserved toasted coconut

Heat oven to 350. Toast 1 cup coconut for 5 to 7 minutes. Reserve ½ cup for frosting. Grease and flour 13 x 9-inch pan. In a large bowl, blend cake mix, water, ½ cup pineapple juice, oil, ¼ cup rum and egg whites at low speed until moistened; beat 2 minutes at *highest* speed. Stir in ½ cup coconut. Pour into prepared pan.

Bake at 350 for 25 to 35 minutes or until toothpick inserted in center comes out clean. Cool 10 minutes. In a small saucepan, heat ½ cup pineapple juice and sugar to boiling. Using long-tined fork, prick cake at ½-inch intervals. Pour hot pineapple mixture over the cake. Cool completely. In a small bowl, blend frosting and 1 tablespoon rum. Frost cake; sprinkle with ½ cup reserved coconut. Serve chilled. 12 servings.

*To substitute for rum, use ¼ cup water and 1 teaspoon rum extract.
Ms. Jeanne Bruns   **Tuscon, Arizona**
The Pillsbury Company   **Minneapolis, Minnesota**

Apricot Brandy Pound Cake

1 cup butter or margarine
3 cups sugar
6 eggs
3 cups sifted flour
¼ teaspoon soda
½ teaspoon salt
1 cup dairy sour cream

1 teaspoon orange extract
½ teaspoon rum extract
¼ teaspoon almond extract
½ teaspoon lemon extract
1 teaspoon vanilla
½ cup apricot brandy

Cream together butter and sugar until light and fluffy. Add eggs one at a time, beating thoroughly. Sift together flour, soda and salt. Combine sour cream, all flavorings, and brandy. Add the flour and sour cream mixtures alternately to the sugar mixture. Mix just until blended. Turn into a 10″ tube pan which has been greased and floured on the bottom. Bake at 325°F for 1 hour and 10 minutes or until cake shrinks from the sides of the pan. Cool in pan about 15 minutes and turn out on wire rack to cool completely. Serves 12.

"It can be frozen. It is delicious with whipped cream flavored with apricot brandy. (1 cup of whipped cream + 1 tablespoon apricot brandy)."
Pat Rice Prideaux   **Rolling Hills High School, Rolling Hills Estates**

Marble Chiffon Cake

⅓ cup unsweetened cocoa
2 tablespoons sugar
¼ cup water
2 tablespoons vegetable oil
2 cups unsifted all-purpose flour
1 ½ cups sugar
3 teaspoons baking powder

1 teaspoon salt
½ cup vegetable oil
7 egg yolks
¾ cup cold water
2 teaspoons vanilla
7 egg whites
½ teaspoon cream of tartar

Combine cocoa, 2 tablespoons sugar, ¼ cup water, and 2 tablespoons oil in a small bowl; stir until smooth. Set aside.

Combine flour, 1 ½ cups sugar, baking powder and salt in large mixer bowl. Add, in order, ½ cup vegetable oil, egg yolks, ¾ cup water and vanilla. Beat at low speed until combined, then at high speed 5 minutes.

With second set of beaters, beat egg whites in a large mixer bowl with cream of tartar until stiff peaks form. Pour batter in a thin stream over entire surface of egg whites; fold in lightly by hand.

Remove ⅓ batter to a separate bowl; gently fold in chocolate mixture. Pour half the light batter into an ungreased 10-inch tube pan, top with half the dark batter. Repeat layers; with narrow spatula, swirl gently through batters to marble. Bake at 325 for 65 to 70 minutes or until done. Invert cake in pan; cool thoroughly. Loosen cake from pan; invert onto serving plate. Glaze with Vanilla Glaze, if desired. 12 servings.

Vanilla Glaze: Heat ¼ cup butter or margarine in saucepan until melted. Stir in 2 cups confectioners' sugar, 1 teaspoon vanilla and 2 to 3 tablespoons hot water or until desired consistency. Pour on top of cake allowing some to run down sides.
Hershey Foods Corporation   *Hershey, Pennsylvania*

Cocoa Apple Cake

3 eggs
2 cups sugar
1 cup margarine
½ cup water
2 ½ cups flour
2 tablespoons cocoa
2 teaspoons soda

1 teaspoon cinnamon
1 teaspoon allspice
1 cup chopped nuts
½ cup chocolate chips
2 apples, grated (2 cups)
1 tablespoon vanilla
Powdered sugar, optional

Beat together eggs, sugar, margarine, water until fluffy. Sift together flour, cocoa, soda, cinnamon and allspice. Add to creamed mixture; mix well. Fold in nuts, chocolate chips, apples and vanilla until evenly distributed. Spoon into greased and floured tube pan. Bake at 325°F for 60-70 minutes or until it tests done. Serves 10.

"Wonderful dusted with powdered sugar or just plain."
Nanci Burkhart   *Hueneme High School, Oxnard*

Marilyn's Cocoa Apple Cake

3 eggs
2 cups sugar
2 sticks margarine
½ cup water
2 ½ cups flour
2 tablespoons cocoa
1 teaspoon soda

1 teaspoon cinnamon
1 teaspoon allspice
2 cups grated apples
1 cup finely chopped walnuts
¼ cup semi-sweet chocolate bits
1 teaspoon vanilla

Cream together until fluffy eggs, sugar, margarine, and water. Sift flour, cocoa, baking soda, cinnamon and allspice. Add to creamed mixture and mix well. Fold in apples, walnuts, chocolate pieces. Add vanilla and mix until distributed evenly. Spoon into a greased & floured 10" loose-bottom tube pan. Bake in 325°F oven 60-70 minutes . . . until cake tests done. Serves 12.

Kathleen Daudistel   *Hanford High School, Hanford*

Whole Wheat Pound Cake

½ pound margarine or butter
2 cups sugar
1 - 1 ½ teaspoons real vanilla

5 eggs
1 cup whole-wheat flour (pastry)
1 cup all-purpose flour

Beat butter or margarine till light and fluffy. Beat in sugar, slowly. Add eggs, one at a time. Beat well. Add flour slowly and beat well. Pour into tube pan. Bake at 350°F for 1 hour. (Be sure pan is greased and floured). Let cool 15 minutes before removing from pan. Does not need frosting. Serves 12.

"My daughter's choice for her birthday cake."
Deanne Moody   *Monte Vista High School, Spring Valley*

German Torte

1 ⅓ cube of butter or margarine
½ cup sugar
1 egg
grated lemon peel and juice

¾ cup flour
1 teaspoon baking powder
2-3 large apples, peeled and sliced
  in thin wedges

Combine butter and sugar and beat until creamy, then stir in egg and grated lemon peel. Sift together flour and baking powder and add gradually to mixture. Grease and flour a springform pan and press dough into the pan. (Add flour as necessary to keep dough from sticking to hands). Arrange apple slices in concentric circles on the crust and sprinkle with a few drops of lemon juice. Bake at 350°F about 45 minutes or until crust is golden brown. Serves 6-8.

Betty M. Williams   *East Bakersfield High School, Bakersfield*

Rum Chocolate Torte

1 Angel food cake
4 tablespoons rum (or more)
4 6-oz. semi-sweet chocolate chips
2 pints whipping cream
6 eggs
2 teaspoons vanilla

dash salt
1 pint whipping cream
6 teaspoons sugar for cream
Toasted slivered almonds
Shaved semi-sweet chocolate, optional

Tear cake into pieces, sprinkle with rum and toss. Melt chocolate in top of a double boiler. Turn into beater bowl and add eggs, one at a time, beating at medium speed. Beat in vanilla and salt. Whip one pint of cream adding sugar. When almost whipped, fold into chocolate mixture. Layer cake and chocolate mixture into a 10" tube pan, greased with butter. Freeze until firm. Frost cake with whipped cream and garnish with almonds and shaved semi-sweet chocolate if desired. Return to freezer until 30 minutes before serving or serve at once. Serves 20.

Jan Keane   *Corona Del Mar High School, Corona Del Mar*

Microwave German Chocolate Cake

¼ cup milk
¼ cup butter

1 pkg. Betty Crocker
    Coconut-Pecan Frosting Mix
1 pkg. Betty Crocker
    German Chocolate Cake

Mix frosting as follows: Put ¼ cup milk and ¼ cup butter in a large batter bowl. Microwave for 1 minute until butter is melted. Empty contents of box into milk-and-butter mixture and mix until well blended. Pour the frosting into the bottom of a large bundt pan. Spread evenly around the bottom of the pan. (No need to grease pan). Mix cake according to directions on the box. EXCEPT use only 1¼ cups water. Pour batter over top of frosting. Microwave on 70% power for 16 minutes. Take out of oven and let set 5 minutes on counter top — not on rack. Invert on cake plate. Serves 10.

Marilyn Pereira   *Hanford High School, Hanford*

Yummy Microwave Carrot Cake

1 ½ cup sugar
1 cup oil
1 teaspoon vanilla
3 eggs
1 ½ cup unsifted flour
¾ teaspoon salt

2 ½ teaspoon cinnamon
1 ¼ teaspoon soda
2 ¼ cups grated raw carrots
¾ cup chopped walnuts
½ cup raisins

In a large mixing bowl, mix sugar, oil and vanilla. Add eggs, beat well. Combine flour, salt, cinnamon and soda. Stir into egg mixture. Fold in carrots, walnuts and raisins. Pour into a 12 x 7" glass baking dish which has been greased on bottom only. Cook on high for 14-15 minutes, giving dish one-half turn every 4 minutes. Cool. Frost with cream cheese frosting:

Cream Cheese Frosting:

3 tablespoons margarine
½ 8-oz. pkg. cream cheese
½ lb. powdered sugar

1 teaspoon vanilla
½ cup chopped walnuts

Cream margarine and cream cheese. Add powdered sugar. Beat until smooth. Add vanilla. Fold in walnuts. Spread on cooled 12 x 7" cake.

"This microwaved cake is very moist and quick to make."
Roberta Baker   **Fontana High School, Fontana**

Benjamin's Apple Crunch

2 cans apple pie filling
1 box yellow cake mix

2 sticks butter (not margarine)
2 3-oz. packages sliced walnuts

In a 13 x 9 x 2" glass pan spread the apple filling. Sprinkle cake mix evenly over apple filling. Slice butter into strips and place over the cake mix. Sprinkle the walnuts over entire mixture, bake at 375°F for 1 hour or until cake mix is golden brown. Serves 10-12.

"This recipe is from James Benjamin, an English Teacher, and it is a favorite of the entire faculty."
Linda L. Zeigler   **Jefferson Jr. High School, Long Beach**

Apricot Upside-Down Cake

1 cube butter
1 cup brown sugar
1 cup flour
1 ½ teaspoons baking powder
3 egg yolks
1 cup granulated sugar

5 tablespoons apricot juice
3 egg whites
¼ teaspoon salt
1 quart canned apricots
1 cup walnut halves

Melt butter in a 10" black cast iron fry pan. Stir in brown sugar, and cook over low heat until "caramelized" (about 5-8 minutes). (Keep over super-low heat until ready to place apricots in.) Meanwhile, sift together flour and baking powder. Set aside. Beat egg yolks until lemony colored, and add 1 cup granulated sugar, and the apricot juice. Mix until well blended. Set aside. Beat egg whites with salt until stiff peaks form. Mix yolk mixture into dry ingredients. Fold beaten whites into batter. Place apricots round side down into caramel. Place walnut halves into caramel round side down. Alternate apricots and walnuts for design. Pour batter over caramel and apricots. Bake in preheated oven 350°F for 40 minutes. Invert cake from pan onto serving platter *immediately* upon removal from oven so cake doesn't stick to pan. Serves 10-12.
Denise D. Tierney   **Ventura High School, Ventura**

Bavarian Apple Torte

Base:
½ cup butter or margarine
¼ cup sugar
½ teaspoon vanilla
1 cup flour

Topping:
2 cups apple, peeled and sliced
¼ cup sugar
1 teaspoon vanilla
½ cup chopped nuts

Filling:
8 ounces cream cheese
¼ cup sugar
1 egg
½ teaspoon vanilla

Combine base ingredients. Mix well. Spread onto the bottom of a 9" pie pan or an 8" square cake pan. Combine filling ingredients and pour on top of base. Combine topping except for chopped nuts and spread on top of filling. Sprinkle chopped nuts over topping. Bake at 375°F for 45 minutes. Serves 8.

'Can be served warm or cold. May be frozen for future use. Combination of apple and cream cheese offers a delicious taste sensation!''
Jeannie Burns
Los Osos Junior High School, Los Osos

Angel Food Dessert

1 Angel food 2-step cake mix
½ pint whipping cream
2 tablespoons sugar

½ teaspoon vanilla
4 large Butterfinger bars

Prepare Angel food cake according to package directions. Bake in ungreased cookie sheet with sides (11 x 17" approx.) at 350°F for 15 minutes or until lightly browned. (Any extra batter can be put in an 8 x 8" pan). Cool. Whip ½ pint whipping cream with sugar. Add vanilla. Frost cooled cake, or use prepared Cool Whip. Freeze Butterfinger bars, crush into chunks with a hammer and sprinkle over the top. Keep refrigerated. Alternate serving suggestions: Use crushed peppermint candy, or Heath bars. Serves 12-16.

"This is a super-quick and easy dessert."
Glenell Fuller
Glendora High School, Glendora

Pumpkin Roll

3 eggs
1 cup sugar
⅔ cup pumpkin
1 teaspoon lemon juice
¾ cup flour
1 teaspoon baking powder
2 teaspoon cinnamon
1 teaspoon ginger

1 teaspoon nutmeg
½ teaspoon salt
1 cup chopped walnuts
1 cup powdered sugar
2- to 3-oz. cream cheese
4 tablespoons butter or margarine
½ teaspoon vanilla

Beat eggs for 5 minutes on high speed. Gradually add sugar, then pumpkin with lemon juice. Mix all dry ingredients together. Add dry ingredients to the egg, pumpkin mixture. Pour into a greased jelly roll pan (10 x 15 x 1"). Pan may be lined with waxed paper instead. Spread chopped nuts on top. Bake 20 minutes at 375°F. Turn on towel sprinkled with powdered sugar. Roll cake and towel together. Cool.

After cake is cooled, unroll cake and fill with icing: beat until smooth the powdered sugar, cream cheese, butter and vanilla. Spread icing on pumpkin bread, roll again. Refrigerate. (Overnight improves flavor).

Betty Ann Lawson   *Valencia High School, Placentia*

Pizza Cake

1 yellow cake mix
1/4 cube butter
2 eggs
1/4 cup brown sugar
1/4 cup water
1/2 cup nuts (chopped)
1 can mandarin oranges
1 can fruit cocktail

1 can pineapple chunks
2 bananas
1 pkg. strawberries
2 tablespoons cornstarch
1/2 teaspoon sugar
1/4 teaspoon cinnamon
2 large containers of Cool Whip
Coconut

Mix cake mix, butter, eggs, brown sugar and water. Add nuts. Grease and flour a 16" and a 12" pizza pan. Spread on batter and bake at 350°F for 12-15 minutes. Drain canned fruit and save 1 1/2 cups juice. Bring to a boil the juice and 2 tablespoons cornstarch, 1/2 teaspoon sugar and 1/4 teaspoon cinnamon. Cook until thick, but will still pour. Cover *cooled* cake with Cool Whip and top with fruit. Sprinkle with coconut and drizzle with *cooled* sauce. Serves 12-16 or more.

"Cake can be frozen."
Nancy Byrum   *Patrick Henry High School, San Diego*

Cherry Chocolate Top

1 pound powdered sugar
3 tablespoons Cocoa
very light sprinkle of salt
3 tablespoons maraschino cherry juice
1 whole egg

2 rounded teaspoons soft butter
1/4 teaspoon vanilla
1 cup maraschino cherries, cut in half
1 cup chopped nuts — walnuts or your choice

Sift together in mixing bowl powdered sugar, cocoa, and salt at slow speed; add cherry juice, egg, butter, and vanilla. Mix well at medium speed. With wooden spoon carefully stir in cut cherries and nuts. Spread mixture over cake immediately when it comes from the oven (heat from oven cooks the egg).

Very good on chocolate or devils food cake that has been baked in a "brownie" pan, cut in squares and left in the pan till serving time. Makes enough for 1 cake.

Ame Lea Middleton   *Yuba City High School, Yuba City*

Buttermilk Fudge Cake

2 cups flour
2 cups sugar
1 cube margarine
½ cup shortening
1 cup water
4 tablespoons cocoa
2 eggs, slightly beaten
½ cup buttermilk
1 teaspoon cinnamon
1 teaspoon soda
1 teaspoon vanilla

Icing:
1 cube margarine
⅓ cup buttermilk
4 tablespoons cocoa
1 pound powdered sugar
1 teaspoon vanilla
1 cup nuts, chopped

Mix flour and sugar and set aside. Beat margarine, shortening, water, cocoa and bring to a boil. Pour into flour and sugar; stir. Add eggs, buttermilk, cinnamon, soda and vanilla. Pour into a greased and floured cookie sheet pan with 1 inch sides. Bake at 350°F for 20 minutes. Five minutes before cake is done, start icing:

Icing: melt margarine, buttermilk, cocoa, and bring to a boil. Add sugar, vanilla and nuts. Mix and spread over hot cake. Serves 15-20.

"Freezes well."
Myra Cochran   *Yuba City High School, Yuba City*

Coca-Cola Cake Frosting

¼ cup margarine
2 tablespoons cocoa
3 tablespoons coca-cola
½ cup miniature marshmallows

½ box powdered sugar
½ teaspoon vanilla
½ cup walnuts

Heat margarine, cocoa and coca-cola to boiling. Stir in marshmallows until dissolved. Beat in sugar and vanilla. Stir in nuts. Spread over warmed cake.
Terri Pratt   *Sage School, Palmdale*

Mrs. Masumiya's Pineapple Frosting

1 20-oz. can crushed pineapple
1 large box vanilla pudding
  (regular, not instant)

1 ½ cups milk
1 carton Dessert Whip

Drain pineapple well. Make pudding as directed using 1½ cups milk. Cool pudding, stirring often to prevent lumps from forming. Set aside. Whip Dessert Whip until stiff. Fold Dessert Whip into cooled pudding. Fold in drained pineapple. Spread on cooled cake. Frosts 2-layer cake.

"For chocolate frosting, omit pineapple and use chocolate pudding."
Reiko Ikkanda   *South Pasadena High School, South Pasadena*

Chocolate Cheese Chip Cupcakes

3 cups sifted flour
2 cups sugar
½ cup cocoa
2 teaspoons soda
1 teaspoon salt
2 cups water
⅔ cup oil

2 tablespoons vinegar
1 teaspoon vanilla
1 8-oz. pkg. cream cheese
1 egg
⅓ cup sugar
1 6-oz. pkg. chocolate chips

In a large bowl, sift together flour, 2 cups sugar, cocoa, soda, and salt. Add water, oil, vinegar, and vanilla. Beat well. In a small bowl, combine cream cheese, egg, and ⅓ cup sugar. Stir in chocolate chips. Fill muffin cups one-half full with chocolate batter. Top each with spoonful of cream cheese mixture. Bake at 350° for 30 minutes. Makes 3 dozen.

"These are delicious! They stay moist up to 5 days."
Sally Scoggin   *Home Economist, Glendora*

Devil's Dump Cupcakes

1 ½ cups flour
½ cup cocoa
1 cup sugar
1 pinch salt
1 pinch baking soda

2 ½ teaspoons baking powder
1 cup cold water
⅔ cup oil
2 eggs
1 teaspoon vanilla

Sift together dry ingredients. Make a well in center. Add liquid ingredients. Beat well with beater. Pour into muffin tins (fill approximately ⅔ full). Bake in 350°F oven about 20 minutes or until toothpick comes out clean. Cool on cooling rack and then frost.

"Super moist, keeps their freshness for a long while. (Old recipe in the family for many years)."
Dorothy Shirley   *Live Oak High School, Live Oak*

Orange Cream Cheese Frosting

1 3-oz. pkg. cream cheese, softened
1 tablespoon margarine or butter, softened
½ teaspoon grated orange peel

1 ½ cups sifted confectioner's sugar
milk, if needed

In a small mixing bowl, beat cream cheese, margarine and orange peel until light and fluffy. Gradually add sugar, beating until fluffy and of spreading consistency. If mixture is too thick, add 1 to 2 teaspoons milk.
Eudora Mitchell   *Norwalk High School, Norwalk*

Smooth and Creamy Frosting

1 pkg. (4-serving size) Jello brand
  instant pudding and pie filling, any flavor
1 cup cold milk

3 ½ cups thawed Cool Whip non-dairy
  whipped topping

Combine pudding mix and milk in small bowl. Beat slowly with rotary beater, or at lowest speed of electric mixer until well blended, about 1 minute. Fold in whipped topping.

Makes about 4 cups, or enough for two 9-inch layers. Store frosted cake in the refrigerator.

Lois Salisbury   *Mt. View High School, El Monte*

Candies

Oh Henry Bars

⅔ cups melted margarine
1 cup brown sugar
1 cup granulated sugar
4 cups oats

3 teaspoons vanilla
1 6-oz. pkg. chocolate chips
⅔ cup chunky peanut butter

Mix margarine, sugars, oats and vanilla. Press into an 8 inch square greased baking pan. Bake at 350° for 10 minutes. Melt chocolate chips and peanut butter over boiling water or in the microwave. Spread over baked bars; cut while warm and refrigerate. Makes 12-16 bars.

Sally Jean Artz   *Santa Fe Middle School, Monrovia*

Truffles

4 cups heavy cream
2 ½ pounds bittersweet chocolate, chopped
   into small pieces

6 ounces sweet butter
½ to 1 cup liqueur

Simmer cream in saucepan until it boils. Remove from heat; add chocolate. Whisk in butter. Divide batch and add different liqueurs for flavor. Chill. Form into balls. Freeze. Dip in chocolate glaze. You can roll in powdered cocoa before freezing if you don't glaze. Makes 4 dozen + .

"This is comparable to Godiva and better than Cocolot."
Dianne Dalzell   *Bakersfield High School, Bakersfield*

English Toffee

1 cup butter
1 cup sugar
¼ cup water

1 12 oz. pkg chocolate chips
1 cup walnuts, chopped

Combine butter, sugar and water. Cook until mixture reaches hard crack stage (300°F), stirring constantly. Pour onto greased cookie sheet. Place chocolate chips on top. Press nuts on top. Cool and crack into small pieces.

Ellen Derby   *Tierra Del Sol School, San Diego*

Caramel Delights

1 14-oz. package caramels
1 cup Eagle Brand milk
¼ pound (1 stick) margarine

1 pkg. large marshmallows
chopped nuts or coconut or Rice Krispies

Combine the caramels, milk, margarine in the top of a double boiler; heat over medium high heat until melted, stirring often. Dip marshmallows in the warm mixture, roll in the nuts, coconut or crushed rice krispies.

Emily Lewis   *Cerritos High School, Cerritos*

Chocolate Meringue Kisses

3 egg whites
¾ cup sugar
3 cups crushed corn flakes

½ teaspoon salt
1 teaspoon vanilla
6 oz. chocolate chips

Beat egg whites till foamy. Add sugar slowly, 1 tablespoon at a time, and beat until you have a very stiff meringue. Fold in corn flakes, salt, vanilla, and chocolate chips. Spoon onto greased brown paper and bake at 350° for 10-15 minutes. Makes approximately 2 dozen kisses.

"Delicious meringue cookie!"
Jennifer Hemstreet   *Santa Maria High School, Santa Maria*

Preposterous Peanut Brittle

2 cups sugar
1 cup light corn syrup
4 tablespoons water

1 cup margarine
2 cups raw peanuts
½ teaspoon baking soda

In a heavy 2-quart saucepan heat sugar, corn syrup, and water. Stir to dissolve sugar over medium-high heat. When mixture boils, lower to medium heat; add butter and stir. Continue to cool slowly. Stand candy thermometer in mixture and after it reaches 230°F stir constantly. When temperature reaches 280° add peanuts all at once and stir rapidly and constantly until temperature reaches 305°F. Remove from heat, add soda, and stir quickly as mixture foams. Pour immediately onto buttered cookie sheets. Crack and wrap when cooled. Serves 16.

"Perfect way to say "thank you" or give as a gift. Pieces can be put into plastic bags and tied with pretty ribbons."
Mary E. Richmond   *San Luis Obispo Senior High School, San Luis Obispo*

"See's" Fudge

In a Heavy Bottomed Pan Place:
2 cups sugar
⅔ cup evaporated milk
10 marshmallows

In a Bowl Place:
1 cup chopped nuts
1 cube margarine
1 teaspoon vanilla
6 ounces chocolate chips

Bring pan ingredients to a rolling boil. Boil for 7 minutes stirring constantly. Be accurate of time. Pour over contents of bowl and blend until smooth. Pour into lightly greased foil lined 8-9" square pan. Cool. Score and cut after pulling candy in foil from pan. Makes 24 pieces.

"If you can read a clock, this is no-fail! More people compare this to the candy fudge — hence the name."
Dianne Dalzell   *Bakersfield High School, Bakersfield*

Toffee

½ pound butter
1 cup sugar
1 tablespoon water
1 teaspoon vanilla

½ cup chopped nuts, if desired
½ Hershey chocolate bar
3 tablespoons nuts, finely chopped

Place butter, sugar and water in a heavy saucepan. Cook at a rolling boil for ten minutes, until mixture turns a rich brown, stirring constantly. Remove from heat and add vanilla and nuts. Pour into a 9 x 9″ pan.

Place ½ Hershey bar on top of hot mass. When softened, spread and sprinkle nuts on top. It is wise to "mark" candy before it hardens. Makes 16 pieces.

Madelyn V. Fielding   *Jordan High School, Long Beach*

2 Minute Microwave Fudge

1 pound box confectioner's sugar (3 ½ cups
   sifted)
½ cup cocoa
¼ cup milk

pinch salt
½ cup butter
1 teaspoon vanilla
½ cup chopped nuts

In a one-quart glass casserole, add powdered (confectioner's) sugar, cocoa, milk, salt and butter. Cook 2 minutes on high. Stir to blend ingredients. Add vanilla and nuts and blend well. Line a pie plate evenly with waxed paper. Pour fudge into plate, and chill until firm.

"You can add any kind of nuts (peanuts, walnuts, etc., or miniature marshmallows if desired)."

Linda Robinson   *Sinaloa Junior High School, Simi Valley*

Cosmic Crunchies

4 ½ cups puffed brown rice cereal
¼ cup pumpkin seeds
¼ cup sesame seeds
¼ cup sunflower seeds
¼ cup almonds
¼ cup raw peanuts, lightly toasted

½ cup coconut (optional)
*1 cup rice syrup
3 tablespoons sesame oil
1 tablespoon vanilla

*available in health food stores

Mix all of the dry ingredients in a bowl that is large enough to toss ingredients together without overflowing. Heat rice syrup to soften, then add the oil and vanilla and stir well. Prepare a jelly roll pan by lining it with foil and oiling the foil. Pour the syrup mixture over the dry ingredients and mix until all the dry ingredients are coated. Spread onto the foil-lined pan and press to flatten. Bake in a 325° oven for about 20 to 25 minutes or until lightly browned. Remove from oven, allow to cool. Peel off the foil and break into chunks. Store in an airtight container to keep crisp.

"Will not work in the microwave. Cannot freeze. But does hold up well for several weeks. This is candy, but a not-too-sweet health treat!"

Mary Boldi   *Vernon Junior High, Montclair*

Feathery Fudge

⅔ cup soft butter or margarine
1 ¾ cup sugar
2 eggs
1 teaspoon vanilla
2 ½ (1 ounce each) squares unsweetened
    chocolate, melted and cooled

2 ½ cup cake flour (2 cups + 1 tablespoon
    regular flour), sifted
1 ¼ teaspoon soda
½ teaspoon salt
1 ¼ cup ice water

Cream butter, sugar, eggs and vanilla for 5 minutes. Add melted, cooled unsweetened chocolate. Sift flour, soda and salt. Add alternately to cream mixture with 1 ¼ cup ice water. Bake at 350°F for 30-35 minutes. Makes one 9 x 13″ or two 8 or 9″ cakes.

Linda Boyd   **Claremont High School, Claremont**

Peanut Butter Balls

1 cube margarine, melted
1 jar peanut butter (14-16 oz.)
1 lb. powdered sugar
3½ cups Rice Krispies

¼ bar paraffin
6-oz. pkg. chocolate chips
1 large Hershey bar (about 4 oz.)

Mix butter, peanut butter and powdered sugar. Add Rice Krispies and mix well. Form into 1-inch balls. Refrigerate if made on a warm day. Melt paraffin, chips and Hershey bar in top of double boiler. Be very careful not to get drops of water or steam into chocolate pan. Put ball onto fork, dip into chocolate. Lift up and down several times to get excess chocolate off. Set on waxed paper or foil until chocolate sets up. They keep better in the refrigerator than at room temperature. They will freeze well also. To save extra dipping chocolate, cover tightly and refrigerate.

"Dipping chocolates really is not difficult and these are super-good!"
Polly Frank   **Lakewood High School, Lakewood**

English Toffee

1 cup sliced almonds
1 cup butter
1 cup granulated sugar
⅓ cup dark brown sugar (packed)

2 tablespoons water
1 tablespoon baking soda
2 cups semi-sweet chocolate chips

Sprinkle almonds in a buttered 13 x 9″ jelly roll pan. In large heavy saucepan melt butter; add sugars and water; mix well. Stir constantly. Place thermometer in mix and boil to 300° (hard crack stage). Remove from heat, stir in soda. Work fast, pour carefully over almonds in pan. Sprinkle chocolate chips over top of toffee and spread evenly as it melts. Chill in refrigerator at least 1 hour. Break into pieces. Makes 1 ½ pounds.

"Candy can be frozen."
Linda L. Zeigler   **Jefferson Junior High School, Long Beach**

Peanut Butter Cups

1 cup powdered sugar
¾ cup peanut butter
2 tablespoons melted margarine

1 cup semi-sweet chocolate chips
2 tablespoons grated paraffin wax

Mix powdered sugar, peanut butter, and margarine together until well blended. Melt chocolate chips and wax in the top of a double boiler. Form peanut butter mixture into ½ inch balls. With a small metal spoon dip each ball into melted chocolate, coating evenly, then place balls on wax paper to cool. If dipping chocolate becomes too thick, reheat, then continue dipping. Candies may be placed in paper candy cups and should be stored in the refrigerator. Makes 3 dozen.

"Requires no baking!"
Jo Anne Bugh   **Rialto Junior High School, Rialto**

Peanut Butter Squares

2 sticks margarine
1 (18 ounce) jar creamy peanut butter
1 pound box confectioner's sugar

1 ½ cups graham cracker crumbs
1 12-oz. pkg. chocolate chips
 (melted)

Melt margarine. Add peanut butter, sugar and graham cracker crumbs. Mix very well. It is quite stiff. Spread and put in a 13 x 9" pan. Spread melted chocolate chip pieces over mixture. Cover. Refrigerate until hard. To cut into 1-inch squares, let stand at room temperature for ½ hour before cutting to prevent cracking. Keep refrigerated.

"Tastes like those great peanut butter cups you buy!"
Betty Muszynski   **Signal Hill School, Long Beach**

English Toffee

1 pound butter
2 cups sugar

1 cup chopped almonds, toasted
1 large Hershey bar, melted

Melt butter and add sugar. Cook until it has reached hard-crack stage when dropped in cold water (color will be golden brown). Remove from heat and add almonds. Pour onto a cookie sheet. When candy sets but before oil hardens, pour off oil. When set, ice with melted chocolate and sprinkle with chopped walnuts. Let icing set. Break into pieces.

Sherril Stubblefield   **Judkins Intermediate School, Pismo Beach**

Carmel Corn (Microwave)

4-6 cups popcorn
½ cup margarine

½ cup brown sugar
7 large marshmallows

Pop corn. Pick out hard kernels. In a 1 ½ quart bowl combine other ingredients. Cook 2 ½ minutes on full power in microwave. Stir until it is a syrup. Cook 30 seconds more. Pour over popcorn and stir. Spread out on waxed paper. Cool.

Janet Griffith   **Norco Senior High School, Norco**

Cheese-cakes

Calorie Watchers Cheesecake

2 tablespoons butter
¾ cup graham cracker crumbs
1 8-oz. pkg. Neufchatel cheese
  (low-fat cream cheese)
¼ cup sugar
1 egg
½ teaspoon vanilla

Topping:
1 cup plain yogurt
2 tablespoons sugar
½ teaspoon almond extract or vanilla

Microwave butter in 8″ glass baking dish until melted (40 seconds). Stir in graham cracker crumbs. Press over bottom and one inch up the side of dish.

For filling: microwave cheese in glass bowl ½ - 1 minute or until softened. Beat in sugar, egg and vanilla. Pour into crust. Microwave uncovered 4-5 minutes at 50% power or until set around edges, rotating dish once.

Combine topping ingredients. Carefully spoon over cheesecake, spreading to cover. Microwave, uncovered 3-4 minutes at 50% power or until heated. (Topping will still be very soft). Refrigerate 3-4 hours or until set. 8 servings.

"About 150 calories per serving. Serve with fresh strawberries or other fruit in season."
Angie Garrett   **Tenaya Middle School, Fresno**

Cheesecake

3 cups fine graham cracker crumbs
⅔ cup brown sugar
⅔ cup melted butter
1 teaspoon ground cinnamon
3 8-oz. pkgs. cream cheese

4 eggs
1 cup sugar
1 teaspoon vanilla extract
1 cup sour cream

Have cheese and eggs at room temperature. Mix first four ingredients well. Reserve 3 tablespoons of this mixture for topping. Press remainder of mixture into two 8″ square cake pans with the back of a spoon. Cream cheese until soft; add eggs, one at a time, beating well after each addition. Add sugar and vanilla, and beat until blended. Pour into shell; bake 35 minutes at 350°F or until firm. Spread top with sour cream and sprinkle with reserved crumbs. Cool; then chill. Serves approximately 30. Yields two 8 x 8″ pans.

Netta Roberts   **Wilson High School, Long Beach**

Company Cheesecake

1 ¼ cups graham cracker crumbs
2 tablespoons sugar
3 tablespoons melted butter
2 8-oz. pkgs. cream cheese
1 cup sour cream

1 cup sugar
2 teaspoons grated lemon peel
¼ teaspoon vanilla
3 eggs

Mix graham cracker crumbs, 2 tablespoons sugar and melted butter together. Press evenly into a pie dish. Bake at 350°F for 10 minutes. Cool completely.

Beat cream cheese in large bowl with sour cream. Gradually add 1 cup of sugar. Beat till fluffy. Add lemon peel and vanilla. Beat in eggs, one at a time. Pour into cooled pie crust. Bake for 1 hour at 300°F. Cool to room temperature and chill for at least 3 hours. Serves 12.

Mary Tatro   *Clifton Middle School, Monrovia*

Diet Cheesecake

2 tablespoons lemon juice
2 tablespoons water
1 pkg. gelatin
1 egg
⅓ cup sugar
½ cup nonfat milk

1 teaspoon vanilla
2 cups low-fat cottage cheese
2 tablespoons butter
1 cup graham cracker crumbs
2 tablespoons water
1 teaspoon liquid sweetener

Combine lemon juice, water and gelatin in a blender and blend until smooth. Add egg and sugar and blend; set aside. Bring milk and vanilla to boiling point and add to blender mixture along with cottage cheese; blend until smooth, set aside.

Combine butter, cracker crumbs, water and sweetener; press into pie pan. Pour blender mixture into crust and chill in refrigerator for 2 hours. Serves 8.

"185 calories per serving."
Ann Clark,   *Pt. Loma High School, San Diego*
courtesy of Vivian Giarratano

Cheesecake

crumbs from 16 graham crackers
¼ cup butter or margarine
1 tablespoon honey
1 tablespoon flour
16 oz. cream cheese
⅓ cup sugar
4 eggs

1 teaspoon vanilla
juice of 1 lemon
1 teaspoon grated lemon rind
1 pint sour cream
½ cup sugar
1 teaspoon vanilla

Mix together graham crackers, margarine, honey and flour. Press firmly into bottom of a spring form pan. Then blend together cream cheese, ⅓ cup sugar, eggs, vanilla, lemon juice, and grated lemon rind until smooth and creamy. Pour on top of crust and bake for 25 minutes at 375°. Cool. Blend together sour cream, ½ cup sugar and vanilla. Pour on top of cooled filling and bake at 375°F for 5 to 8 minutes. Cover with plastic wrap and refrigerate for at least 12 hours. If cut too soon, top of cheesecake will be runny. Serves 12.

Maxine S. Shepherd   *Moreno Valley High School, Sunnymead*

Gourmet Cheesecake

Crust:
1 ½ cups graham cracker crumbs
5 tablespoons melted butter
1 tablespoon sugar

Topping:
3 cups sour cream
½ cups sugar
1 ½ teaspoon vanilla

Filling:
3 8-oz. cream cheese
5 eggs
1 cup sugar
1 ½ teaspoon vanilla

Mix together and press into a 9 x 13" baking dish, the graham cracker crumbs, melted butter and 1 tablespoon sugar. Blend together with electric mixer the cream cheese and eggs (add eggs one at a time). Slowly blend in the 1 cup of sugar and vanilla. Pour on top of crumb mixture and bake at 300°F for one hour. Let cake stand for 3 minutes. Raise oven temp to 350°F. Spread on topping. Bake 5 minutes. Chill for several hours before serving. Serves 16-20.

"If desired, spread a can of cherry or blueberry pie filling mix on top of cake. Cut into squares to serve.
Nancy Byrum   **Patrick Henry High School San Diego**

Cheesecake Supreme

Zwieback or graham cracker crust
2 envelopes unflavored gelatin
½ cup Kahlua
½ cup water
3 eggs, separated

¼ cup sugar
⅛ teaspoon salt
2 8-oz. pkgs cream cheese
1 cup whipping cream

Prepare crust. In the top of a double boiler, soften gelatin in Kahlua and water. Beat in egg yolks, sugar and salt. Cook over boiling water, stirring constantly, until slightly thickened. Beat cheese until fluffy. Gradually beat in Kahlua mixture; cool. Beat egg whites until stiff but not dry. Beat cream stiff. Fold egg whites and cream into cheese mixture. Pour into prepared pan. Chill 4 or 5 hours before serving. Serves 10-12.
Mary Conant   **Grandview School, Valinda**

German Cheesecake

Crust:
1 ½ cups graham crackers (crushed)
¼ cup sugar
⅓ cup butter or margarine (melted)

Topping:
1 cup sour cream
1 tablespoon sugar
½ teaspoon vanilla

Filling:
2 eggs (separated)
½ cup sugar
1 tablespoon lemon juice
rind of ½ lemon, grated
½ teaspoon vanilla
1 pound cream cheese (cubed)

34

Preheat oven to 375°F. Combine crumbs, sugar and melted butter until well mixed. Press into bottom of 9″ springform pan. Bake 8-10 minutes or until golden brown. Cool. Reduce oven temperature to 300°. Combine egg yolks, sugar, lemon juice and rind, vanilla and half of the cheese in blender container. Cover and process at medium speed until smooth. Remove cover and add remaining cheese gradually, continuing to process until mixture is very smooth. Beat egg whites with rotary beater until stiff. Fold blended mixture into egg whites, pour into crust and bake 45 minutes.

Put sour cream, sugar and vanilla into blender container and process on low speed until smooth. Spread evenly over top of cake and return to oven for 10 minutes. Cool cake and remove rim of springform pan before serving.

Lianne Bennett   *Macy Intermediate School, Monterey Park*

Blueberry Cheesecake

21 graham crackers	2 eggs
½ cup butter	½ cup sugar
¼ teaspoon cinnamon	½ teaspoon vanilla
½ cup cream cheese	1 can blueberry pie mix
8 oz. cream cheese	ice cream or whipped cream

Roll graham crackers to a fine consistency. Put ½ cup butter, ¼ teaspoon cinnamon and ½ cup sugar in bowl and mix. Add to graham crackers and press into bottom of a 9 x 13″ cake pan.

Mix 8 oz. cream cheese, ½ cup sugar and 1 teaspoon vanilla. (Often I double this making more filling). Pour over above mixture and bake for only 20 minutes (no more) at 350°F. Cool well. Add one can of blueberry pie mix over the top and serve with ice cream or whipped cream.

Libby Christensen   *Bernardo Yorba Jr. High School, Yorba Linda*

Cherry Cheesecake

1 pkg. lemon cake mix	1 8-oz. pkg. cream cheese, softened
1 cup water	⅓ cup evaporated milk
4 eggs	1 can (1 pound 5 oz.) cherry pie filling

Generously grease and lightly flour a 10″ tube pan or spray with Pam. In large mixing bowl, combine dry cake mix, water and eggs. Blend and beat as directed on package. Pour about half of batter into prepared pan. In small mixing bowl, beat cream cheese and milk until smooth. Spoon over batter in pan without touching sides of pan. Spoon 1 cup cherries over cream-cheese mixture. Spread with remaining batter. Bake at 350°F for 50-55 minutes, until toothpick inserted in center comes out clean. Cool in pan 15 minutes. Do not invert. Remove from pan. Serve with remaining cherries and spread over top of cake. Store leftover cake in the refrigerator. Serves 16-20.

Barbara Silvey   *Gidley School, El Monte*

My Finest Cheesecake

Crust:
1 ½ cups graham cracker crumbs
3 tablespoons sugar
½ teaspoon ground cinnamon
¼ cup (½ stick) sweet butter, melted

* Lemon Glaze (recipe below)

Filling:
3 8-oz. pkgs. cream cheese
 (room temp)

1 ¼ cups sugar
6 eggs
1 container (1 pint) dairy sour cream
⅓ cup all-purpose flour
2 teaspoons vanilla
grated rind of 1 lemon
juice of ½ lemon

To make the crust: generously grease a 10 x 3" springform pan with butter. Place pan in center of a 12-inch square of aluminum foil and press foil up around sides of pan. Combine graham-cracker crumbs, sugar, cinnamon and melted butter in a small bowl until well-blended. Press 1 ¼ cup of crumbs mixture into bottom and sides of pan. Chill prepared pan while making filling (reserving remaining crumb mixture for topping).

To make filling: with electric mixer on low speed or with a wooden spoon, beat cream cheese in a large bowl until soft. Gradually beat in sugar until light and fluffy. Beat in egg yolks one at a time until well-blended. Stir in sour cream, flour, vanilla, lemon rind and juice until smooth. Beat egg whites until they hold stiff peaks. Fold whites into the cheese mixture souffle fashion, until well-blended. Pour into prepared pan. Bake in moderate oven (350°F) 1 hour and 15 minutes, or until top is golden. Turn off oven heat and allow cake to cool in oven for 1 hour. Remove cake from oven and allow to cool on a wire rack at room temp. Sprinkle remaining crumbs on top or Lemon glaze.

*Lemon glaze: 1 Sunkist lemon, unpeeled, 3 cups water, 1 cup sugar, 2 tablespoons plus 2 teaspoons cornstarch, ⅓ cup fresh squeezed lemon juice, few drops yellow food coloring.

Slice lemon into paper-thin cartwheels, removing any seeds; reserve one slice for garnish. Coarsely chop remaining slices; place in saucepan with two cups water. Combine thoroughly, sugar and cornstarch and blend in remaining 1 cup water until smooth. Add drained lemon juice. Bring to a boil, stirring constantly, boil 3 minutes. Stir in coloring; chill until cool but not set. Spread on cheesecake and garnish with lemon cartwheel twist. Serves 16.

Gwen Hansen   **Bloomington High School, Bloomington**

Cheesecake Tarts

2 8-oz. pkgs. cream cheese
2 eggs
1 tablespoon lemon juice
1 teaspoon vanilla

1 box vanilla wafers
1 pkg. of 2 ½" diameter
 aluminum muffin paper cups
1 can cherry pie filling

Cream together cheese, sugar, eggs, lemon juice and vanilla. Place muffin cups into a muffin tin. Place one vanilla wafer on the bottom of each muffin cup. Fill cups ¾ full with cheese mixture. Bake 15-20 minutes at 375°F. Cool. Top each with cherry pie filling. Serves 10-15.

"Very festive! Great for special occasions!"
Linda Leo   *La Sierra High School, Riverside*

Cheese Cake (With Raspberry Glaze)

Crust:
20 individual graham crackers
3 teaspoons sugar
½ teaspoon cinnamon
⅓ cup butter or margarine, melted

Filling:
2 8-oz. pkgs. cream cheese
2 eggs
¾ cup plus 2 tablespoons sugar
2 teaspoons vanilla
1 tablespoon lemon juice

Topping:
2 cups sour cream
4 tablespoons sugar
2 teaspoons vanilla

Glaze:
1 cup raspberry pulp (fresh or frozen,
  1 package) put through a sieve
½ cup sugar
1 tablespoon cornstarch

Crush graham crackers very fine; add sugar, cinnamon and melted butter. Mix thoroughly and pat into a 10″ springform pan. Cream the cheese in mixer (let cheese stand at room temperature before mixing, for a smoother texture). Add eggs, sugar, vanilla and lemon juice; beat well. Pour into crust and bake at 350°F for 20 minutes. Cool for 5 minutes.

Blend together ingredients for topping. Spread over cooled cheese layer and return to 350°F oven for 5 minutes. Then for glaze: Combine and cook over medium heat the raspberries, sugar and cornstarch, until thick. Stir occasionally. Chill. Cover cake. Chill at least 6 hours. Serves 12-16.

"Cut recipe in half — bake in a 7″ springform pan. Great for small dinner parties!"
Miriam Imlay Phelps   *Palm Springs High School, Palm Springs*

Pineapple Cheesecake

¾ cup graham cracker crumbs
2 tablespoons melted butter
1 8-oz. pkg. softened cream cheese
½ cup sifted confectioner's sugar

1 1 ¼-lb. can crushed pineapple,
  well-drained
1 2-oz. pkg. dessert topping mix

Mix graham cracker crumbs and butter (reserving 2 tablespoons for top); press on the bottom of an 8-inch round cake pan; chill. Whip cream cheese and confectioner's sugar until fluffy. Stir in pineapple. Prepare topping according to package directions; fold into pineapple mixture. Spread over crust. Sprinkle with reserved crumbs; chill well. Serves 6-8.

Jean Jeter   *Park View Intermediate, Lancaster*

Invisible Crust Cheesecake

3 eggs
2 8-oz. pkgs cream cheese
⅔ cup sugar

1 cup sour cream
1 tablespoon vanilla
4 teaspoons sugar

Mix first 3 ingredients in blender or with a mixer. Pour into a buttered glass pie pan. Cook for 30 minutes at 350°F. Cool for 20 minutes. Mix next 3 ingredients and smooth on pie. Bake 10 minutes more. Cool and keep in refrigerator. Serves 8-10.

"You may also add your own fruit glaze or fruit pie filling on top."
Linda Tsutsui   **Hanford High School, Hanford**

Super Simple Cheesecake

12 ounces cream cheese
2 eggs
½ cup granulated sugar
2 teaspoons lemon juice

1 cup sour cream
2 tablespoons powdered sugar
1 teaspoon vanilla
9" graham cracker crust

Soften cream cheese in microwave for 30 seconds. Add eggs and beat well. Add sugar and lemon juice and beat until very fluffy. Pour into prepared graham cracker crust in 9" pie pan. Beat together sour cream, powdered sugar and vanilla. Pour on top of cream cheese mixture. Bake at 325°F for 25 minutes. Cool and serve with favorite fresh fruit topping. Serves 8.

"This is a recipe I developed to use in our Fish & Chip Restaurant called the FISH BOAT in San Luis Obispo that we had for 4 years. Just recently sold it!"
Mary E. Richmond   **San Luis Obispo Senior High School, San Luis Obispo**

Raspberry Cream Cheese Coffeecake

2 ounces cream cheese
¼ cup butter
2 cups Bisquick
⅓ cup milk
½ cup rasberry preserves

Icing:
½ cup powdered sugar
1 tablespoon milk
¼ teaspoon vanilla

Cut cream cheese and butter into Bisquick until crumbly. Blend in ⅓ cup milk. Turn dough onto wax paper and knead 10 times. Roll dough into an 8" x 10" rectangle; turn onto greased cookie sheet. Spread preserves down center. On long sides of rectangle cut through dough to preserves at one-inch intervals. Fold every other strip of dough over preserves. Bake at 425°F for 12-15 minutes. For icing, combine powdered sugar, milk and vanilla. Drizzle over hot coffeecake. Serves 8.

"This is always a class favorite."
Deborah Karr   **Griffiths Middle School, Downey**

Mrs. Smith's Cheesecake

Crust:
20 graham crackers
½ cube butter, melted
2 tablespoons sugar

Topping:
2 cups sour cream
½ cup sugar
1 teaspoon vanilla

*or use standard graham cracker crust

Filling:
2 eggs
½ cup sugar
1 teaspoon vanilla
3 3-oz. pkgs Philadelphia cream cheese
  (room temp)

Crush the graham crackers. Mix with the melted ½ cube butter, and sugar. Press into a 9″ pie pan. Bake at 350°F for 5 minutes.

Beat 2 eggs, ½ cup sugar, 1 teaspoon vanilla into softened cream cheese. Pour into crust. Bake at 350°F for 20 minutes.

Mix the sour cream, sugar, and vanilla. Pour on hot pie. Bake at 350°F for 5 minutes. Refrigerate 3-5 hours (at least 4 hours before serving). Serves 8+.

"Mrs. Smith, the grandmother of one of my girlfriends from the 5th grade, has used this recipe since 1929."
Willy Hall   *McPherson Jr High School, Orange*

Lemon Cheesecake

Crust: ⅓ cup butter
1 ½ cup graham cracker crumbs
¼ cup sugar
1 tablespoon lemon juice
¼ cup finely chopped walnuts
¼ teaspoon cinnamon

Filling:
3 8-oz. pkgs. cream cheese
¾ cup sugar
⅓ cup heavy whipping cream
2 tablespoons flour
2 tablespoons lemon peel or
2 tablespoons lemon juice
2 tablespoons flour
4 eggs and 3 egg yolks

For Crust: Melt butter, combine with other ingredie nts. Press into a 9″ pie pan. Bake at 350°F until light brown (approx. 15 minutes). Cool.

For filling: In medium bowl, beat cheese until creamy. Add sugar, whipping cream, flour and lemon peel or juice. Beat in eggs one at at time. Pour into cool crust. Bake at 350°F for 50 minutes. Turn off oven and leave cheesecake in oven 30 minutes longer. Cool in pan. Refrigerate. Serves 8.
Vicki A. Hansen   *Tranquillity Union High School, Tranquillity*

Notes

Cookies

Mini Chip Brownies

½ cup butter or margarine
1 cup packed light brown sugar
1 egg
1 teaspoon vanilla

1 cup unsifted all-purpose flour
½ teaspoon salt
1 cup semi-sweet chocolate Mini Chips

Melt butter or margarine in small saucepan; stir in brown sugar. Remove from heat; pour into small mixer bowl. Cool; beat in egg and vanilla until fluffy. Add flour and salt to creamed ingredients. Beat just until well blended; stir in Mini Chips. Spoon into greased 8- or 9-inch square pan. Bake at 350° for 25 to 35 minutes or until toothpick inserted in center barely comes out clean. Cool; frost, if desired. Cut into squares. 16 brownies.

Hershey Foods Corporation   *Hershey, Pennsylvania*

Honey Walnut Brownies

1 ½ cups butter
1 cup honey
1 teaspoon vanilla
1 egg
2 cups whole-wheat pastry flour

½ teaspoon baking powder
½ teaspoon salt
2 cups rolled oats
2 cups chopped walnuts
½ cup chocolate chips (optional)

Cream butter, honey and vanilla. Beat in egg, add flour, baking powder and salt. Beat until smooth. Add oats and walnuts (and chips). Spread evenly in a buttered 8 x 8 x 2" pan. Bake at 350°F oven for 30 minutes until lightly brown. Cool for 10 minutes then cut. (Good cold or frozen also). Makes 16.

Libby Christensen   *Bernardo Yorba Jr High School, Yorba Linda*

Brownies Extraordinary

1 8-oz. pkg. softened cream cheese
⅓ cup sugar
1 egg
¼ teaspoon almond extract
2 1 oz. squares unsweetened chocolate
½ cup Parkay margarine

2 eggs
1 cup sugar
¾ cup flour
½ teaspoon baking powder
½ teaspoon salt
sliced almonds

Combine cream cheese, ⅓ cup sugar, 1 egg, and almond extract. Set aside. Melt chocolate and margarine; cool. Beat 2 eggs and add 1 cup sugar and chocolate mixture. Sift together dry ingredients and add to chocolate mixture. Mix well. Pour half of chocolate batter into a greased 8" pan; spread cream cheese mixture over chocolate; spread with remaining chocolate mixture; sprinkle with sliced almonds. Bake at 350°F oven for 45 minutes. Makes 16-2" squares.

"Old favorite from Kraft Foods."
Donna Long   *South Hills High School, Covina*

Recipe for "Mini Chip Brownies" on page 42 →

Becky's Brownies

1 cup butter
4 oz. unsweetened chocolate
4 eggs
2 cups sugar
1 cup flour
1 cup whole pecans

Frosting:
2 oz. unsweetened chocolate
¼ cup coffee (optional)
3 tablespoons butter
1 tablespoon cream
⅛ teaspoon salt
2 cups powdered sugar

Melt 1 cup butter and chocolate over low heat. Beat the 4 eggs until light; add the 2 cups sugar gradually. Add the flour and mix, then the pecans. Bake in a greased 9 x 13″ pan at 350° for 20-25 minutes. Cool. Makes 24 bars.

For frosting: boil together 2 oz. chocolate, coffee, butter, cream and salt for 3 minutes; then add the powdered sugar. Frost and serve.

"Expensive, but well worth the effort - the best I've ever tasted!"
Glenell Fuller   **Glendora High School, Glendora**

Cargo Squares

1 cup butter or margarine
1 1-lb. box brown sugar
3 eggs
2 teaspoons vanilla
3 cups flour

½ teaspoon salt
3 teaspoons baking powder
2 cups chocolate chips
1 cup nuts

In a 4 qt. saucepan, melt butter. Remove from heat and stir in brown sugar; cool slightly. Using a wooden spoon, stir in eggs and vanilla. Add flour, salt and baking powder; mix well. Stir in chocolate chips and nuts. Spread mixture into a well-greased 10″ x 15″ baking sheet (jelly roll pan). Bake at 350°F for 25 minutes. Cool and cut into squares.

"This recipe feeds a crowd and is very popular with my guests."
Beth Guerrero   **Selma High School, Selma**

Brownies

1 cup margarine
2 cups sugar
¼ cup cocoa

4 eggs
1 teaspoon vanilla
2 cups flour

In a mixing bowl, cream margarine and sugar together, add cocoa and mix well. Add eggs one at a time. Add vanilla and flour; mix until smooth. Spread in a greased and floured 9″ x 13″ baking pan. Bake at 325° for 30 minutes only. Variation: add ½ cup chopped nuts.

"Very moist brownies with a mild flavor."
April Herman   **Ramona Junior High School, Chino**

← Recipe for "Old-Fashioned Chocolate Ice Cream" on page 66

Oatmeal Brownies

2 ½ cups quick-cooking or regular oats
¾ cup flour
¾ cup packed brown sugar
½ teaspoon baking soda
¾ cup margarine (melted)
4 squares unsweetened chocolate
⅔ cup shortening

2 cups sugar
2 eggs
1 teaspoon vanilla
1 ¼ cups flour
1 teaspoon baking powder
1 teaspoon salt

Heat oven to 350°F. Grease baking pan (13 x 9 x 2"). Mix oats, flour, brown sugar and baking soda. Stir in melted margarine. Reserve ¾ cup of the oatmeal mixture. Press remaining oatmeal mixture in pan. Bake 10 minutes; cool 5 minutes. Heat chocolate and shortening in a 3-quart saucepan over low heat until melted; remove from heat. Stir in sugar, eggs and vanilla. Mix in remaining ingredients. Spread dough over baked layer. Sprinkle with reserved oatmeal mixture. Bake until brownies begin to pull away from sides of pan, about 30 minutes. Cool; cut into about 1 ½" squares. Makes 4 dozen cookies.

Peggy Adams   **Paramount High School, Paramount**

No-Bake Brownies

1 cup chopped walnuts
4 cups graham cracker crumbs
½ cup sifted powdered sugar

1 12-oz. pkg semi-sweet chocolate pieces
1 cup evaporated milk
1 teaspoon vanilla

Combine nuts, graham cracker crumbs and sugar in a large bowl. Melt chocolate in evaporated milk over low heat, stirring constantly. Blend well. Add vanilla then set aside ½ cup of the chocolate mixture. Stir the crumb mixture into the remaining chocolate mixture and spread into a well-buttered 9" square pan. Spread remaining chocolate mixture over top. Chill. Cut into 16 squares.

Joanne Fial   **East Middle School, Downey**

Low-Cal Brownies

2 cups fine graham cracker crumbs
½ teaspoon cinnamon
¼ teaspoon salt
1 cup skim milk

1 teaspoon vanilla
½ cup semi-sweet chocolate chips melted
½ cup chopped nuts
1 tablespoon sifted powdered sugar
(optional)

Combine crumbs, cinnamon, and salt. Stir in milk and vanilla, mixing well. Add chocolate and nuts, blend thoroughly. Turn into a lightly greased 9" pan. Bake at 350° for 15 - 20 minutes, or just until done. Turn out on rack to cool. Cut in 40 pieces, sprinkle powdered sugar over top if desired.

"Approx. 44 calories per piece"
Pat Storms   **Anna McKenney Intermediate School, Marysville**

Macaroon Kiss Cookies

⅓ cup butter or margarine
1 pkg. (3 oz.) cream cheese, softened
¾ cup sugar
1 egg yolk
2 teaspoons almond extract
2 teaspoons orange juice

1 ¼ cups unsifted all-purpose flour
2 teaspoons baking powder
¼ teaspoon salt
5 cups (14-oz. pkg.) flaked coconut
1 9-oz. pkg. milk chocolate kisses
  (about 54)

Cream butter or margarine, cream cheese and sugar until light and fluffy. Add egg yolk, almond extract and orange juice; beat well. Combine flour, baking powder and salt; gradually add to creamed mixture until well blended. Stir in 3 cups flaked coconut. Cover dough and chill about 1 hour. Shape dough into 1-inch balls. Roll balls in remaining coconut; place on ungreased cookie sheet. Bake at 350° for 10 to 12 minutes or until lightly browned on bottom. Remove from oven and press a milk chocolate kiss into center of each cookie. Allow to cool one minute. Carefully remove cookies from sheet and cool until chocolate kiss is firm. About 4-½ dozen cookies.

Hershey Foods Corporation   *Hershey, Pennsylvania*

Chocolate Chip Cookies

⅔ cup shortening
⅔ cup butter or margarine, softened
1 cup granulated sugar
1 cup brown sugar (packed)
2 eggs
2 teaspoons vanilla

3 cups all-purpose flour
1 teaspoon soda
1 teaspoon salt
1 cup chopped nuts
2 6-oz. pkgs. semi-sweet chocolate pieces

Heat oven to 375°. Mix thoroughly, shortening, butter, sugars, eggs and vanilla. Blend in remaining ingredients. (For a softer rounder cookie, add ½ cup flour.) Drop dough by rounded teaspoonfuls 2″ apart onto ungreased baking sheets. Bake 8-10 minutes or until light brown. Cool slightly before removing from sheet. Makes 7 dozen.

"Freeze unused dough in a airtight freezer container. Thaw it until just soft enough to spoon onto baking sheet. Both cookie dough and baked cookies can be frozen and stored from 9 to 12 months."

Eudora Mitchell   *Norwalk High School, Norwalk*

Swedish Oatmeal Cookies

2 cubes butter
½ cup sugar

3 cups quick (1 minute) oatmeal

Mix all ingredients together with fingers and form into balls. Press down with fork on greased cookie sheet. Bake in a 325°F oven for 8-10 minutes.

"These cookies come out very flat and crisp!"

Nancy Horn   *Selma High School, Selma*

Forgotten Cookies

2 egg whites, beaten until stiff
⅔ cup sugar
1 pkg. semi-sweet chocolate chips

1 cup chopped walnuts
½ teaspoon vanilla

Add the sugar gradually to the stiffly beaten egg whites, tablespoon by tablespoon, beating again after each addition. Fold in chocolate chips, chopped walnuts and vanilla. Preheat oven (350°F). Prepare cookie sheet with Pam or cut brown paper to fit large cookie sheet. Drop batter with spoon on cookie sheet. Put in oven and turn off the heat. Leave overnight or at least 6 hours without opening door. Makes 3 dozen.

"Recipe contains no salt, no fat and no flour. Excellent choice for people on special diets. A very attractive and tasty cookie. Can also be frozen!"
Pauline S. Jones (retired)

Cabrillo Jr. High School, Ventura

Pecan Thumbprints

1 pound margarine
12 oz. cream cheese
4 cups flour
3 eggs, slightly beaten

2 cups brown sugar
1 teaspoon vanilla
1 tablespoon margarine, melted
1 cup pecans

Combine 1 pound margarine, cream cheese and flour. Roll in balls about half the size of a golf ball. Shape in pan with thumb. Mix eggs, brown sugar, vanilla and melted margarine. Fill pastry cups half way with egg mixture. Sprinkle chopped pecans over top. Bake at 350°F for 25 minutes or until set. Makes 8 dozen small.

"Use tiny tart pans for above recipe or make larger balls for regular muffin cups. Freezes well also."
Mrs. Lois Armstrong

Sonora High School, La Habra

Lily Cookies

4 ½ oz. cream cheese
1 cup butter
2 ½ cups flour

orange marmalade
powdered sugar

In large bowl mix the cream cheese, butter and flour to form a dough. On lightly sugared (with powdered sugar) board, roll dough to about ¼" thickness. Cut with a 2" round cutter. Roll each circle into a cornucopia, on baking sheet, by bringing two rounded edges together, letting them overlap. Press gently. Fill open part of each cookie with about ¼ teaspoonful of marmalade. Bake cookies in 375° oven for 15 minutes. Cool, then drench with sifted powdered sugar.

"Very rich, but light tasting. Go easy on the marmalade — if you put too much on a cookie it runs all over the pan during baking and you have a sticky, gooey mess!"
Donna Neel

Orangeview Junior High School, Anaheim

Chocolate Chip Butter Cookies

1 pound butter or margarine
powdered sugar (2 cups + extra for dusting)
½ teaspoon salt
2 teaspoons vanilla

4 ½ cups flour
1 12-oz. pkg. semi-sweet
    chocolate pieces

Cream together butter and 2 cups powdered sugar. Add salt, vanilla, and flour and mix until blended. Mixture will be stiff. Stir in chocolate pieces. Pinch off pieces of dough. Roll into 1 inch-balls and flatten with a form on baking sheet. Bake at 350°F oven for 15 minutes. Sprinkle with additional powdered sugar while hot. Makes 64 cookies.

"These cookies are very rich and buttery!"
Pam Ford
Rowland High School, Rowland Heights

Mrs. Traw's Sugar Cookies

¾ cup margarine
1 cup sugar
2 eggs
¼ teaspoon vanilla

2 ½ cups flour
1 teaspoon baking powder
1 teaspoon salt
fluffy frosting**

Cream margarine and sugar. Blend in eggs and vanilla. Add flour sifted with baking powder and salt; mix well. *Chill*. Roll ½" thick and cut in desired shapes. Bake on *ungreased* baking sheet at 400°F, 8-10 minutes. Cool. Decorate with Fluffy Frosting:

**Fluffy Frosting: Cream 3 tablespoons margarine, dash of salt and ½ teaspoon vanilla. Add 1 ½ cups sifted confectioner's sugar alternately with 1 tablespoon plus 1 ½ teaspoons milk, beating until fluffy. Tint with food coloring if desired.

"This is the best sugar cookie recipe I have ever used in my classes. Even a beginner can make this recipe work. I use it for Christmas, Easter and Valentine's Day."
Marianne Traw
Ball Junior High School, Anaheim

Peanut Butter Bon Bons

3 cups crushed Wheaties
1 lb. powdered sugar
½ cup butter

2 cups chunky peanut butter
16 oz. semi-sweet chocolate chips
¼-½ cake paraffin wax

Mix crushed Wheaties, powdered sugar, butter and peanut butter with hands. Shape into balls about the size of walnuts. Chill in freezer, 1 hour or longer. Melt the chocolate chips and paraffin in top of double boiler, over low heat. Dip chilled balls into chocolate. Place on wax paper and chill until set. Makes 100 cookies.

"Can be frozen."
Charla Moore
McLane High School, Fresno

Toasted Oatmeal Cookies

2½ cups oats
¾ cup margarine
1 cup brown sugar
1 egg
1 teaspoon vanilla

½ cup flour
1 teaspoon cinnamon
½ teaspoon salt
½ teaspoon baking soda

In a medium skillet, over medium heat, sauté oats in melted margarine until golden, about 5 minutes. Remove from heat. Cool. In large mixing bowl, combine sugar, egg and vanilla. Beat until light and fluffy. Stir in oats and flour, cinnamon, salt and baking soda. Drop by spoonfuls onto cookie sheet. Bake 10-12 minutes in 375° oven. Makes 3 dozen.

Carol Krause   *Alta Loma Junior High School, Alta Loma*

Gobs (cookies with filling)

2 cups sugar
2 eggs
½ cup shortening
1 cup boiling water
1 cup buttermilk
1 teaspoon vanilla

½ teaspoon baking powder
2 teaspoons soda
½ cup cocoa
4 cups flour
½ teaspoon salt

Cream sugar, eggs, shortening; add water, buttermilk, vanilla. Sift together baking powder, baking soda, cocoa, flour and salt. Add to first mixture. Spread out about 1 tablespoon batter on cookie sheet. Bake in over 375°F for 12-13 minutes. Cool and add filling.

Filling: Cook until thick — 1 cup milk, 5 tablespoons flour; chill. Cream ¾ cup shortening–margarine mixed, 1 cup powdered sugar, ½ teaspoon vanilla. Add to chilled mixture and beat. Take two gobs (cookies) and fill them with the filling until all are filled.

Lillian Lee   *Hanford High School, Hanford*

Margarine Oat Crisps

1 cup (½ pound) margarine
½ cup sugar
1 cup unsifted flour

1 ½ cups quick-cooking oatmeal
1 teaspoon almond extract

Cream margarine, add sugar until light and fluffy. Stir in flour, oatmeal and almond extract until well blended. Drop by rounded teaspoonfuls about 2" apart on greased cookie sheet. Bake at 375°F oven until edges are light brown (8 to 10 minutes). Cool slightly on pans; transfer to cooling rack and dust with powdered sugar. Makes 4 doz.

"This is great for children to make — and low in sugar!"
Faye Nielsen   *Rosemead High School, Rosemead*

Angel Drops (Original recipe)

2 egg whites
²/₃ cup sugar, granulated
vanilla flavoring

1 cup chocolate chips
½ cup pecans (optional) chopped

Heat oven to 350°. Beat egg whites to stiff consistency; add sugar *slowly* and continue beating. Fold in vanilla, chocolate chips and pecans. Place by teaspoonfuls on cookie sheet (teflon). They don't grow, so place close together. Place in oven - *TURN OFF OVEN*. When oven is cold, next morning eat!

"You do not have to remember when to take the cookies out of the oven . . . this has saved me . . . I always get so busy and forget; hence, they burn. They can stay in there days, if they last! . . . but not at my house!"

Variations: Raise eggs to 3 egg whites and 1 cup sugar — makes more. OR substitute mint flavoring for vanilla and dye green for St. Patricks Day or Christmas. They are fun to make — & EASY!!"

Gage Jones   *South Pasadena High School, South Pasadena*

Brown Kuchen

²/₃ cup sugar
1 ½ cup molasses
½ cup shortening
2 teaspoons vanilla
½ pound candied fruits
1 cup chopped nut meats

4 cups sifted flour
1 teaspoon soda
1 teaspoon baking powder
½ teaspoon salt
1 teaspoon cinnamon
1 teaspoon cloves

Boil sugar, molasses and shortening for five minutes. Cool. Add vanilla, fruits and nuts. Sift together dry ingredients and stir into first mixture. Form dough into rolls about 2" in diameter. Chill at least 12 hours. Slice and bake on well-greased baking sheet in a moderate 350°F oven for 10-12 minutes. I use Grandma's Molasses. Makes 2 dozen.

"Keep in covered cookie jar (A Swedish recipe)."
Charlene M. Stott   *Horace Mann Junior High School, San Diego*

Quickie Cookies

30 soda crackers (or more to fill pan used)
1 cup butter or margarine

1 cup brown sugar
1 12-oz. pkg chocolate chips

Line large cookie sheet with aluminum foil and grease lightly. Lay crackers on foil. Boil butter and sugar for 3 minutes, stirring constantly. Pour syrup over crackers. Bake at 350°F for 5 minutes. Remove from oven and sprinkle with chocolate chips. When chips are soft spread with rubber spatula. Cool and separate.

Sandra French   *Long Beach Unified School District, Long Beach*

Chinese Sweet Crescents

2 tablespoons toasted sesame seeds
½ cup chopped salted peanuts
½ cup coconut flakes
½ cup brown sugar

½ cup granulated sugar
1 pound pkg won ton skins
1 egg, beaten
oil for deep frying

In small skillet, toast sesame seeds until golden brown. Cool. Place sesame seeds in medium bowl with chopped peanuts, coconut flakes, brown sugar, granulated sugar and mix well. Prepare won ton skins by folding them into triangles and then trimming off the 4 corners with scissors to form circles. Place a teaspoon of filling in center. Moisten edges with beaten egg and seal. Deep fry in hot oil until golden brown, turning once. Drain. Cool. Store in airtight container. Makes 6-7 dozen.

"These will keep for 3-4 weeks in an airtight container. Unused won ton wrappers will keep in the refrigerator up to 7-10 days or in the freezer for up to 3 months. If frozen, defrost before using."
Brenda Wong   *Yuba Gardens School, Olivehurst*

Rocky Road Fudge Bars

Bar:
½ cup butter
1 oz. unsweetened chocolate
1 cup sugar
1 cup flour
½-1 cup chopped nuts
1 teaspoon baking powder
1 teaspoon vanilla
2 eggs

Frosting::
2 cups miniature marshmallows
¼ cup butter
1 oz. unsweetened chocolate
2 oz. reserved cream cheese
¼ cup milk
3 cups powdered sugar
1 teaspoon vanilla

Filling:
8 oz. cream cheese (reserve 2 oz.)
2 tablespoons butter
½ teaspoon vanilla
½ cups sugar
1 egg
¼ cup chopped nuts
6 oz. chocolate chips

Heat oven to 350°. Grease and flour a 13" x 9" pan. In a large pan over low heat, melt ½ cup butter and chocolate. Add remaining bar ingredients. Mix well. Spread in prepared pan. In small bowl, combine 6 oz. cream cheese with all filling ingredients, but chocolate chips and nuts. Beat 1 minute at medium speed until smooth and fluffy: stir in nuts. Spread over chocolate mixture. Sprinkle with chocolate chips. Bake for 25 to 35 minutes. Remove from oven; sprinkle with marshmallows. Bake 2 minutes longer. In large saucepan, over low heat, melt ¼ cup butter, 1 oz. chocolate, remaining 2 oz. cream cheese and milk. Stir in powdered sugar and vanilla until smooth. Immediately pour over bars, store in refrigerator.
Barbara Parks   *Clovis West High School, Fresno*

Ladyfingers or Barney Googles

1 recipe Feather Cake (see below)   jar of salted peanuts (ground)
chocolate powdered sugar frosting

After cake has cooled, freeze it for several hours to make handling easier.

Cut cake into long slender pieces, approximately 1" wide x 4" long. Using your favorite chocolate powdered sugar icing which has been thinned to pouring consistency, pour it over the cake slices so all sides are coated. Roll in ground salted peanuts. (Makes approximately 20-30 bars).

Feather Cake:
1 cup shortening
2 cups granulated sugar
3 cups sifted pastry (cake) flour
2 teaspoons baking powder

¾ teaspoon salt
1 teaspoon vanilla, almond or lemon extract
1 cup milk
6 egg whites

Cream shortening and sugar. Sift together flour, baking powder and salt. Add extract to milk. Add slowly and alternately the milk and dry ingredients, beating constantly. Beat egg whites until stiff. Fold egg whites into batter. Pour into greased and floured pans. (This amount makes three 8" - 9" layers or one 9 x 13" and one 8" - 9" layer). Bake at 350°F for 25-30 minutes.

"Cake mixes do not work as well as the Feather Cake recipe as they have more of a tendency to crumble. My mother made these, and called them ladyfingers. Once about 35 years ago, I saw similar ones in a small cafe called Barney Googles. They are unusual and delicious."
Helen Sarviel   **Lewis Jr. High School, San Diego**

Pumpkin Squares

1 pkg. yellow cake mix
  (reserve 1 cup for topping)
½ cup melted butter or margarine
1 egg
1 large can pumpkin (3 cups)
¾ cup sugar
2 eggs

1 teaspoon vanilla
1 small can evaporated milk
sprinkle of cinnamon
¼ cup sugar
1 teaspoon cinnamon
¼ cup soft butter or margarine
½ cup chopped nuts

Mix cake mix, ½ cup melted butter or margarine and 1 egg together, and spread over the bottom of a greased 13 x 9" pan. Combine pumpkin, ¾ cup sugar, 2 eggs, vanilla and sprinkle of cinnamon; beat until well blended. Pour over bottom layer. Combine 1 cup reserved cake mix, sugar, 1 teaspoon cinnamon, ¼ cup soft butter and chopped nuts and sprinkle over top of filling as a streusel topping. It is not crumbly. May have to drop by teaspoon.

Bake at 350°F for 45-50 minutes. It does not have to be quite set until knife comes clean as is the case for pumpkin pie.

"Tasty when served with whipped cream or ice cream."
Priscilla Bechok   **Bell Gardens High School, Bell Gardens**

Raspberry Chews

1 ½ cups flour
1 ½ cups rolled oats
1 cup coconut
1 cup chopped almonds
1 cup brown sugar
½ cup butter (softened)
2 tablespoons water

Filling:
2 10-oz. pkgs. frozen red raspberries
   (thawed)
2 ½ tablespoons cornstarch
½ teaspoon lemon juice

Heat oven to 350°F. Lightly spoon flour into measuring cup; level off. In large bowl, combine all crust ingredients; mix well. Press half of mixture in bottom of ungreased 13 x 9″ pan.

In small saucepan, combine raspberries and cornstarch. Heat to boiling, stirring constantly. Boil gently 2 minutes or until thickened. Cool; stir in lemon juice.

Pour raspberries over crust, sprinkle with remaining crust mixture. Bake at 350°F for 35-40 minutes or until light brown. Makes 36 bars.

"I serve it as a Christmas bar cookie. It stores well in the refrigerator for about 3 weeks. Do not microwave it!"

Sue Nall

Temple City High School, Temple City

Chewy Delights

1 ½ cups graham cracker crumbs
1 6-oz. pkg. chocolate chips
1 6-oz. pkg. butterscotch morsels

1 14-oz. can sweetened condensed milk
1 cup walnuts (chopped)

Combine all ingredients and stir well. Press mixture into a greased 9″ square pan. Bake 25-30 minutes in a 350°F oven. Makes 3 dozen.

Cari Maze Sheridan

Dexter Intermediate School, Whittier

Chocolate Chip Cheese Squares

2 pkgs. refrigerated chocolate
   chip cookies
2 eggs
½ cup sugar

½ teaspoon vanilla
2 8-oz. pkgs. cream cheese
   (room temperature)

Slice 1 package chocolate chip cookies and place in the bottom of a 13 x 9″ pan. Pat down to fit pan. Mix together eggs, sugar, vanilla, cream cheese. Spread mixture on cookie mixture. Slice second package of cookies and place on top of batter. Do not pat down. Bake at 350°F for 25-30 minutes. Cool and cut into squares.

Betty Muszynski

Signal Hill School, Long Beach

Chinese Chews

2 cups flour
1 cup butter or margarine
1 cup brown sugar
1 ½ cups brown sugar
2 tablespoons flour

¼ teaspoon salt
1 cup coarse chopped pecans
2 eggs
1 teaspoon vanilla
½ teaspoon baking powder

Mix to crumbs flour, butter and 1 cup brown sugar. Put in a 9 x 13" pan. Bake 10 minutes at 300°F. Remove and spread with 1 ½ cups brown sugar, flour, salt, pecans, eggs, vanilla and baking powder. Beat together well, and spread over the baked crust. Bake 300° for about 30-40 minutes. Cool and cut into squares.

"These can be frozen."
Liz Douglas   ***Newton Junior High School, Hacienda Heights***

Cheese Apple Squares

1 ½ cups flour
1 ½ cups graham cracker crumbs
1 cup packed brown sugar
½ teaspoon baking soda
¾ cup butter or margarine, softened
6 slices processed American Cheese

4 cups peeled, thinly sliced cooking apples
1 cup granulated sugar
½ teaspoon cinnamon
¼ teaspoon nutmeg
½ cup walnuts, chopped

Blend flour, crumbs, brown sugar and soda; cut in butter until crumbly; reserve 1 ½ cups for topping; press remainder in bottom of 13 x 9 x 2" baking pan. Arrange cheese slices over crumb crust, spread apples evenly over cheese; sprinkle with combined granulated sugar and spices. Combine nuts with reserved crumbs; sprinkle over apples. Bake at 350°F for 40-45 minutes until apples are tender. Serves 10-12.

"Can be frozen."
Andrea Roberts   ***Apply Valley Jr. High School, Apple Valley***

Lemon Cheese Bars

1 yellow pudding cake mix
1 egg
⅓ cup oil
1 8-oz. pkg. of cream cheese

⅓ cup sugar
1 tablespoon lemon juice
1 egg

Mix dry cake mix, 1 egg and oil until crumbly, reserve 1 cup. Pat remaining mixture lightly in an ungreased 13 x 9 x 2" pan. Bake 15 minutes at 350°F.

Beat cream cheese, sugar, juice, and 1 egg until light and smooth. Spread over baked layer. Sprinkle with reserved crumb mixture. Bake 15 minutes more. Cool. Cut into bars. Serves 20-24.

"Easy to do and very tasty. Can be frozen."
Leona L. Rice   ***Ahwahnee Middle School, Fresno***

Date Pin Wheels

Filling:
2 ¼ cups chopped dates
1 cup granulated sugar
1 cup water
1 cup chopped nuts

Cookie Dough:
1 cup shortening
2 cups brown sugar
3 slightly beaten eggs
4 cups sifted flour
½ teaspoon salt
½ teaspoon baking soda

Simmer dates, sugar and water for about 10 minutes or until thick. Add nuts and let cool. Cookie Dough: Cream shortening and brown sugar. Add eggs and beat until light and fluffy. Add the dry ingredients, sifted together. Mix well. Chill several hours. Divide dough in half and roll each into a rectangle until scant ¼ inch. Spread with date mixture. Roll as for a jelly roll. Chill overnight. Slice about ¼" thick and bake in 400°F oven for 10-12 minutes. Makes 5 dozen.

Joanne S. Fields   *La Sierra High School, Riverside*

Graham Cracker Cookies (Toffee)

48 graham crackers (one inner package)
1 cup brown sugar
1 cup butter

1 cups nuts (slivered almonds)
1 large Hershey chocolate bar

Butter a jelly roll pan. Line the pan with graham crackers. Boil together for 2 minutes the brown sugar and butter in a saucepan. Pour the sugar/butter mixture over the crackers. Sprinkle the nuts over this. Bake at 350°F oven for 7-8 minutes. Break the Hershey bar into small pieces over the top while hot. When melted, spread chocolate evenly over the top. Cut into squares while hot. Cool in freezer. Makes 4 dozen.

Carolyn Crum   *Newhart School, Mission Viejo*

Caramel Layer Choco Squares

1 14-oz. pkg. light caramels
⅓ cup evaporated milk
1 chocolate cake mix (17 ½ oz.) dry
¾ cup softened butter or margarine

⅓ cup evaporated milk
1 cup chopped nuts or peanuts
1 (6 oz.) pkg. chocolate chips

Melt caramels and ⅓ cup evaporated milk together; set aside. Grease a 9 x 13" pan. Combine dry cake mix, butter, ⅓ cup evaporated milk, and nuts. Stir by hand until dough holds together. Press ½ on bottom of pan. Bake at 350°F for 6 minutes. Sprinkle chips over hot dough. Spread caramel mixture over chips. Crumble remaining dough over caramel mixture. Return to oven and bake 15-18 minutes. Cool slightly, refrigerate about 30 minutes. Then cut into squares.

"Don't overcook. Stays gooey."
Kim Frost   *Corcoran High School, Corcoran*

Cherry Walnut Chewies

½ cup butter (1 stick), melted
2 cups yellow cake mix
½ cup coconut flakes

1 ½ cups walnuts, coarsely chopped
1 cup candied cherries, sliced
1 14-oz. can condensed milk (Bordens)

In a 9 x 13" pan, melt the butter and spread it evenly over the bottom. Now layer and sprinkle *evenly*, the cake mix, coconut flakes, walnuts, and sliced cherries. Drizzle the condensed milk evenly all over. Bake in a 350°F oven for about 25-30 minutes, or until top is golden brown.

Allow to cool in the pan for about 25 minutes. When still warm, but can be handled easily, cut into 1 ½-inch squares and remove from pan. Place cookies on a brown paper bag. When cool, ever so lightly, sprinkle with some powdered sugar. Makes 48 cookies.

"Cookies freeze beautifully. Freeze in double plastic bags. Remove from bag when defrosting. Store cookies in an airtight container. This recipe is so easy but really tasty. Everybody's favorite!"
Bonnie Smith   **Tustin High School, Tustin**

Butterscotch Bars

½ cup butter or margarine
2 cups packed brown sugar
2 eggs
1 teaspoon vanilla
2 cups all-purpose flour

2 teaspoons baking powder
¼ teaspoon salt
1 cup shredded coconut
1 cup chopped walnuts

In a saucepan (2-quart) melt butter or margarine and brown sugar and cook over low heat until bubbly, stirring constantly. Cool. Add eggs, one at a time, beating well after each addition. Stir in vanilla. Stir together flour, baking powder and salt. Add to brown sugar mixture with coconut and nuts; mix well. Spread in greased 15½" x 10-½" x 1 inch baking pan. Bake at 350° about 25 minutes. Cut into bars while still warm; remove from pan when almost cool.

"Should be stored in airtight container so cookies do not dry out, should be moist and chewy."
Marie Humphrey   **Grant School, Escondido**

Apricot Bars

1 ½ cups flour
1 ½ cups oatmeal
1 cup sugar
1 cup finely chopped nuts

½ teaspoon salt
1 teaspoon baking powder
1 cup melted butter or margarine
2 cups apricot jam

Blend all dry ingredients. Add melted butter. Press ⅔ of mixture into a 9 x 13 x 13" pan. Spoon apricot jam evenly over mixture in pan. Spoon remaining mixture over jam. Bake at 375°F for 40-45 minutes. Cool and cut into bars.
Clyle Alt   **Bell Gardens High School, Bell Gardens**

Lemon Treats

2 cups flour
½ cup powdered sugar
1 cup butter (the real thing)
4 eggs

2 cups sugar
5 tablespoons lemon juice
grated rind of 2 lemons
powdered sugar

Pre-heat oven to 350°F. Mix flour and powdered sugar together in small mixing bowl with electric mixer. Add butter and mix. Pat the mixture into a 9 x 13" baking pan. Bake in pre-heated oven for 20 minutes. While mixture is baking, beat eggs, gradually add sugar, lemon juice and lemon rind. Pour the beaten mixture over hot crust. Bake 20-25 minutes at 350°F. *Dust* with powdered sugar after removing from oven. Cool 4 hours in refrigerator or cool overnight. Cut into squares and ENJOY! Makes 3 dozen.

"Tip: Grate only the yellow outer skin of the lemon. The white will be bitter!"

"P.S. This delicious treat was served to me in the recovery room at Scripps Hospital, and I had to get the recipe (Modified)."
Alice F. Mittermiller   *La Jolla High School, La Jolla*

Marshmallow Fudge Bars

Bars:
¾ cup flour
¼ teaspoon baking powder
2 tablespoons cocoa
½ cup Crisco shortening
¾ cup sugar
2 eggs
1 teaspoon vanilla
½ cup nuts
miniature marshmallows

Icing:
½ cup brown sugar
½ cup chocolate chips or 2 squares chocolate
¼ cup water
3 tablespoons margarine
1 teaspoon vanilla
¼ cup powdered sugar

Mix all bar ingredients, excluding marshmallows. Place in a greased 9 x 12" pan. Bake at 350°F for 20-25 minutes. Remove from oven and cover with mini-marshmallows. Return to oven for 3 minutes. Watch carefully. Frost. Makes 24 squares.

Icing: Bring to a soft boil the first 3 icing ingredients. Let boil for 3 minutes. Add 3 tablespoons margarine and 1 teaspoon vanilla. Blend in ¼ cup powdered sugar. Let cool 5-10 minutes and then frost bars.

"Excellent treat and very well liked They also freeze okay."
Vicki A. Pearl   *Giano Intermediate School, La Puente*

Frozen Specialties

Coconut Surprise

3 quarts Baskin-Robbins Coconut Ice Cream
½ cup semi-sweet chocolate chips
1 tablespoon light cream
1 shredded wheat biscuit, crumbled
1 quart Baskin-Robbins Chocolate Ice Cream

1 ½ quarts fresh fruit:
    fresh sliced strawberries
    peeled orange pieces
    fresh pineapple chunks
    fresh sliced banana
    green grapes
    (or other fruit in season)

Line two 2-quart bowls with plastic wrap (or use one bowl and go through process twice). Line each bowl with 1 ½ quarts of slightly softened coconut ice cream to create a shell. Freeze until very firm.

Melt chocolate chips with cream. Add shredded wheat to chocolate. Cool to room temperature. Stir mixture into softened chocolate ice cream. Invert coconut ice cream shells onto a board or tray. Remove plastic wrap. Frost the outside of each shell with the chocolate mixture. Freeze ½ hour to firm slightly. Run the tines of a fork through the chocolate coating in a random manner to create a textured look. Freeze.

Cut one coconut shell in half (make a jagged edge if desired). Set other coconut shell upright on serving tray or platter. Top with the larger portion of the cut shell, creating an opening in front. Smooth out line where shells connect and use fork to replace texture on chocolate surface. Freeze. Prepare fruit salad and chill thoroughly. Just before serving, fill coconut shell with chilled fruit. Set smaller portion of shell, if desired, chocolate side down on tray next to large shell for additional servings. Garnish tray with more fresh fruit and fresh mint if desired. Very spectacular! Makes 16 to 24 servings.

Ms. Sherrol Nicklas
Baskin-Robbins Ice Cream

Rocky River, Ohio
Glendale, California

Jamoca Volcano

1 pint Baskin-Robbins Jamoca Almond
   Fudge Ice Cream
½ pint (1 cup whipping cream)
2 tablespoons sugar

1 tablespoon cocoa
½ teaspoon vanilla
Irish Whiskey, Brandy or Rum
Cinnamon

Make four large scoops of ice cream. Using the handle of a long-handled wooden spoon, or similar tool, bore a hole, about 2' deep, into each scoop. Freeze until firm.

Whip cream with sugar, cocoa and vanilla. (This may be prepared and refrigerated for several hours before serving.)

Fill each of four stemmed goblets or tulip sundae dishes ½ to ⅔ full of chocolate whipped cream. Set scoops of ice cream into whipped cream so that opening is upright. Fill each opening with Irish Whiskey. Top scoops with remaining whipped cream. Dust with cinnamon and serve. Makes 4 sundaes.

Ms. Miriam Cohen
Baskin-Robbins Ice Cream

Cambridge, Massachusetts
Glendale, California

Ice Cream Sopaipillas

1 ½ cups flour
1 teaspoon baking powder
¼ teaspoon salt
¼ cup vegetable shortening
½ cup water

1 jar (10 to 12 oz.) caramel topping
cinnamon sugar (1 tablespoon cinnamon to
½ cup sugar)
1 quart Baskin-Robbins Pralines 'n Cream
chopped pecans (optional)

Mix flour, baking powder and salt together. Cut in shortening until mixture is the size of small peas. Gradually add water to flour mixture, until all is moistened. Knead dough until smooth. Place in bowl, cover and refrigerate one hour to overnight.

On a floured cloth or surface, roll dough into a 6-inch x 12-inch rectangle. Divide into eight equal squares, then cut into 16 triangles.

Fill deep fat fryer with enough oil to at least cover dough pieces. Heat to 400°. Fry triangles one or two at a time. While frying, gently tap top of dough with a fork or spatula until it puffs into a high pillow shape. Continue to turn and fry until golden brown. Carefully place on paper towel covered cooling racks. Cool to room temperature.

Warm caramel topping. Combine sugar and cinnamon. Open side of each triangle and insert a narrow slab of ice cream. Arrange two sopaipillas on each dessert plate, top with warm caramel topping, sprinkle with sugar-cinnamon mixture and garnish with pecans (optional). Makes 8 servings.

Mr. Jerry Rossett
Baskin-Robbins Ice Cream

Houston, Texas
Glendale, California

Deluxe Fruit Ice Cream

2 ripe medium bananas, cut up
1 pint fresh strawberries, hulled
2 cups pitted chopped fresh apricots
1 cup orange juice
½ cup lemon juice

*3 cups milk
*2 cups sugar
2 cups whipping cream
¼ teaspoon salt

In a blender container, place bananas, strawberries, apricots, orange juice, and lemon juice; cover and blend at medium speed until smooth. Turn mixture into large bowl. In same blender container, place milk, sugar, cream and salt; cover and blend till smooth. Stir milk mixture into fruit mixture. Turn into 4-quart ice cream freezer container; freeze according to manufacturer's directions. Makes 3 ½ quarts.

*Substitute the following to make *delicious* Frozen Fruit Yogurt:

1 ½ cup honey for sugar, 2 quarts plain yogurt in place of milk and cream.

"The freezer container should not be more than ⅔ full of the ice cream mixture before mixing. This allows room for the incorporation of air."
Sydney Fox

Orange Glen High School, Escondido

Gram's Lemon Sherbet

1 quart milk
2 cups sugar
pinch of salt

3 lemons, squeezed
1 tablespoon lemon rind

Combine milk, sugar, salt, lemon juice and rind. Freeze in automatic ice cream freezer or refrigerator freezer. Serves 8-10.

"This was a recipe from my husband's grandmother. It originated in the mid-1800s and is still delicious and simple. Can be doubled, tripled, etc."
Jane McPhee   *Fountain Valley High School, Fountain Valley*

Hampshire Peach Ice Cream

1 egg
1 cup (½ pint) sour cream
1 cup whipping cream
1 cup sugar

2 tablespoons lemon juice
½ teaspoon vanilla
2 cups diced fresh peaches, about 4-5
    medium sized peaches

Turn freezer control to coldest setting. Beat egg in large bowl; blend in remaining ingredients. Pour into baking dish or trays and freeze. When ice crystals begin to form, turn into bowl and beat with electric mixer to consistency of soft mush. Return to freezer container and freeze. Repeat two or three times for best texture. NOTE: This may also be made in a mechanical ice cream freezer. Fill freezer container with ice cream mixture and freeze according to freezer instructions. Makes 6 to 8 servings.
Amber Bradley   *El Capitan High School, Lakeside*

Ice Cream with Kumquats and Crimson Sauce

1 10-oz. pkg. frozen raspberries,
    thawed
2 tablespoons sugar
½ teaspoon lemon juice

½ teaspoon brandy extract or 1 tablespoon
    brandy
3 dozen kumquats
½ gallon vanilla ice cream

In an electric blender, puree the raspberries and sugar. Force the raspberry mixture through a strainer to remove seeds. Add lemon juice and brandy. Set aside. Slice kumquats crosswise 1/16" thick. Spoon ice cream into serving dishes. Top each serving with 2 tablespoons of raspberry topping. Garnish with kumquats.
Martha Ford   *Roosevelt Junior High School, Glendale*

Ice Cream Calabasas

oil
flour tortillas

cinnamon and sugar mixture
vanilla ice cream

Heat about ½ inch of oil in an electric skillet at 400°F. When oil is hot gently slip in a flour tortilla with tongs. Fry just a few seconds on each side. Remove and drain on paper toweling. Put fried tortilla on a plate, sprinkle with the cinnamon and sugar mixture, top with ice cream and serve.

"Quick, easy recipe that is delicious!"
Jane Brooks   **Calabasas High School, Calabasas**

Ginger Sundae Sauce

⅓ cup light corn syrup
¼ cup very finely minced crystalized ginger
dash salt

½ cup half and half cream
¼ cup butter (not margarine)
½ teaspoon vanilla

Mix corn syrup, ginger, salt and ¼ cup cream in sauce pan. Simmer 10-15 minutes, stirring until thickened slightly. Gradually stir in remaining cream to ginger mixture. Heat thoroughly but do not boil. Remove from heat and stir in butter and vanilla. Makes ¾ cups.

"May be served warm over vanilla ice cream and sprinkled with toasted almonds. Can be made ahead of time and stored in refrigerator. Reheat to serve but if heated too long may carmelize."
Sharon Schooping   **El Dorado High School, Placentia**

Chocolate Mousse

½ cup cream
½ cup milk
½ cube margarine
1 small pkg semi-sweet chocolate chips

2 tablespoons rum
½ teaspoon instant coffee
2 eggs

Heat cream and milk in a saucepan until scalded. Mix margarine, chocolate chips, rum, instant coffee and eggs in a blender for five minutes. Pour milk and cream slowly into blender. Mix two minutes. Pour in glasses and set in freezer for 1 hour. Remove to refrigerator until serving time. Serves 6.

"Delicious — melts in your mouth!"
Doris Waller   **Chino High School, Chino**

Almond Torte

2 cubes butter
2 cups light brown sugar
2 eggs
10 tablespoons (½ cup and 2 tablespoons flour)

1 teaspoon almond extract
1 cup pecans, chopped
1 cup almonds, chopped
½ pint whipping cream
2 tablespoons powdered sugar

Cream butter until light and fluffy. Gradually add sugar. Beat in the 2 eggs and the flour. Add almond extract. Stir in pecans and almonds. Shape into a roll and wrap in aluminum foil. Freeze for at least 3 hours. Remove from freezer a few minutes before serving. Slice and serve topped with whipped cream and powdered sugar. Serves 8

Pam Amelotte   *Ocean View High School, Huntington Beach*

Val's Pineapple Walnut Dessert

1 pkg. (7 ½ oz.) vanilla wafers
1 cup butter
1 cup sugar
2 eggs
2 teaspoons vanilla

2 cups grated pineapple, well drained
1 cup finely chopped walnuts
whipped cream, walnuts, and maraschino
*   cherries for topping*

Crush vanilla wafers to fine crumbs. Cream butter, adding sugar gradually while continuing to cream. Add eggs one at a time, beating well after each addition. Add vanilla and mix. Combine pineapple and walnuts.

Line an 8 x 5 x 3" loaf pan with foil, leaving overhang so loaf can be lifted out easily.

Press ½ cup vanilla wafer crumbs on bottom of pan. Add about ¼ pineapple mixture; spread evenly. Repeat until mixtures are used up, ending with pineapple mixture.

Chill at least 24 hours or freeze. Garnish with whipped cream, walnuts, and maraschino cherries. Slice and serve. Serves 10-12.

Sheila Dauphin   *John Glenn High School, Norwalk*

Coconut Macaroon Dessert

1 pint whipping cream
3 tablespoons sugar
1 teaspoon vanilla
1 box coconut macaroons (about 24 cookies)

½ cup nuts, chopped fine
1 pint orange sherbet
1 pint pineapple sherbet
1 pint raspberry sherbet

Whip cream and add 3 tablespoons sugar and vanilla. Crumble macaroons to a fine texture and mix with nuts. Add to whipped cream mixture.

Place a layer of whipped cream mixture in the bottom of 9 x 13" dish. Top with a layer of orange sherbet (slice entire pint of sherbet). Top orange sherbet with another layer of whipped cream, then top with layer of pineapple sherbet, a layer of whipped cream and finally a layer of raspberry sherbet. Top with a layer of whipped cream and freeze.

Upon serving, you can garnish with maraschino cherries and nuts.

"Any combination of sherbets may be used. For example — orange, pineapple, lime."
Sylvia Kassap   *Paramount High School, Paramount*

Raspberry Macaroon Freeze

1 pkg. soft macaroon cookies,
   torn in pieces (about 2 cups)
½ cup chopped walnuts

½ pint whipping cream,
   whipped and sweetened
2 pints raspberry sherbet

Fold cookie pieces and nuts into whipping cream. Spread half of cookie mixture over the bottom of a 9″ square pan. Cut sherbet into thick slices and place on top of mixture in an even layer. Spread remaining cookie mixture over top. Cover with plastic wrap and freeze. Serve in squares. Serves 10-12.

"Great to keep in freezer to serve on the spur of the moment!"
Sandra Massey   **Mt. View High School, El Monte**

Frozen Banana Split

1 cup graham cracker crumbs
½ cup sugar
½ cup melted butter
6 oz. semi-sweet chocolate chips
½ cup butter
2 cups powdered sugar

½ cup evaporated milk
3-4 bananas
½ gallon vanilla ice cream
½ pint whipping cream, whipped
nuts

Mix together cracker crumbs, sugar and melted butter. Pat into greased 9 x 13″ pan. Chill in freezer 45 minutes. Melt over low heat chocolate chips and ½ cup butter. Stir in powdered sugar and evaporated milk. Cook until slightly thickened. Cool. Slice bananas over crust and chill in freezer 45 minutes. Spread ice cream over banana layer and freeze 45 minutes. Pour chocolate sauce over ice cream and freeze 45 minutes. Spread whipped cream over chocolate sauce, sprinkle with nuts and freeze until serving time. Serves 12.
Carole Delap   **Golden West High School, Visalia**

Butter Pecan Dessert

2 cups Ritz Cracker crumbs
1 stick margarine, melted
2 pkgs. (small) instant vanilla pudding
2 cups milk

1 quart butter pecan ice cream, softened
2 pkgs. Dream Whip
4 Heath bars (freeze) crushed
   (break in package with hammer or mallet)

Mix cracker crumbs and margarine in a 9 x 13″ glass dish. Press on bottom of pan.

Mix pudding with milk as directed on package. Add ice cream and mix together. Spread mixture over crumbs and freeze. Prepare Dream Whip as directed and fold in 3 of the crushed Heath bars. Spread over filling. Sprinkle remaining Heath bar over top of filling.

"This special dessert is delightful for its ease in preparation and its keeping quality in the freezer. The rich crust is always a real surprise when the ingredient is revealed."
Kathleen DeBelius   **Mt. View High School, El Monte**

Frozen Lemon Crumb Dessert

½ cup flour
2 tablespoons brown sugar
¼ cup butter
¼ cup finely chopped pecans
2 eggs, separated

1 ⅓ cups (14 oz.) sweetened condensed milk
⅓ cup fresh or bottled lemon juice
1 ½ teaspoons grated lemon rind
3 tablespoons sugar

Mix flour, brown sugar, butter and pecans until crumbly. Spread on cookie sheet lined with aluminum foil. Bake in 350°F oven until crisp and golden 13-15 minutes. Stir occasionally to break up crumbs. Cool. Line ice cube tray with heavy-duty foil, leaving a 1 ½ inch collar around edges. Spread ⅔ of crumb mixture in bottom. Beat egg yolks until thick and lemon colored. Blend in condensed milk. Add lemon juice and rind; stir until thickened. Beat egg whites until stiff but not dry. Gradually beat in 3 tablespoons sugar; fold into lemon mixture. Pour crumbs in pan; sprinkle with reserved crumbs. Freeze until firm. When solid, lift from tray and cover with a piece of foil large enough to seal liner. Press liner and cover edges together; fold up and over to seal. Label and return to freezer. Cut into bars to serve. Makes 6 servings.

"This is a great make-ahead dessert for company!"
Nancy Bryant   **Buena Park High School, Buena Park**

Lime Delight

1 ½ cups crushed Ritz crackers
¼ cup sugar
½ cup margarine or butter
½ gallon vanilla ice cream
2 pints lime sherbet

¼ cup lemon juice
1 cup sugar
6 tablespoons butter or margarine
2 eggs

Mix together crushed crackers, sugar, and butter. Press into a 9 x 13" pan. Soften ice cream and sherbet. Mix well and pour over cracker crust. Freeze. Cook lemon juice, sugar and margarine over low heat until well blended. Beat eggs well. Add to lemon juice mixture and continue cooking until thickened. Cool. Pour over frozen ice cream mixture. Freeze. Serves 12.

Sue Hope   **Lompoc Valley Middle School, Lompoc**

Frozen Orange Crunch

1 cup almonds (browned)
2 ½ cups Rice Chex (rolled)
¼ cup butter or margarine, melted
¾ cup brown sugar

1 cup coconut
1 gallon ice milk
1 cup orange juice concentrate

Brown almonds; crush Rice Chex. Melt margarine. Stir in almonds, Rice Chex, brown sugar and coconut. Put ⅔ of this mixture on the bottom of a 13 x 9 x 2 inch pan. Mix ice milk and orange juice concentrate together. Pour over crust. Sprinkle remaining ⅓ of crust mixture over the top. Freeze. Serves 15.

Joretta Stewart   **Olive Junior High School, Baldwin Park**

Butterscotch Crunch Squares

1 cup flour
¼ cup quick cooking oatmeal
¼ cup brown sugar
½ cup butter or margarine

½ cup chopped nuts
1 12 oz. jar caramel ice cream topping
½ gallon chocolate ice cream

Combine flour, oatmeal and brown sugar; cut in butter or margarine till mixture resembles coarse crumbs. Stir in nuts. Pat mixture into a 13 x 9 x 12 inch baking pan. Bake in a 400° oven for 15 minutes. Stir while warm to crumble; cool. Spread half the crumbs in 9 x 9 x 2 inch baking pan, drizzle about half the ice cream topping over crumbs. Stir ice cream to soften; spoon carefully into pan. Drizzle with remaining topping and sprinkle with remaining crumbs. Freeze. Serves 9-12.

"The crumbled cookies would make a good topping for any flavor sundae. This is from Better Homes magazine and is a family favorite."
Judith C. Betz   *Greenfield Junior High School, Bakersfield*

Frozen Strawberry Squares

½ cup butter
1 cup flour
¼ cup brown sugar
½ cup chopped nuts

2 egg whites
1 tablespoon lemon juice
1 cup sugar
16 oz. frozen strawberries

Melt butter in a 9 x 13" pan. Combine flour, brown sugar, and nuts; pour over melted butter and spread in pan. Bake at 350°F for 20 minutes. Remove from oven and cool. Save ½ cup of crumbs for topping. Prepare "mile high filling": put egg whites, lemon juice, sugar and strawberries (thawed) in a large bowl. Beat for 25 minutes on high speed with an electric mixer. Spread filling over crumb base in a 9 x 13" pan, sprinkle reserved ½ cup topping over filling. Freeze 2 hours before serving. Serves 12.

"A very light dessert."
April Herman   *Ramona Junior High School, Chino*

Freezer Ice Cream

2 cups sugar
6 eggs
1 can sweetened condensed milk
1 pint whipping cream
1 pint half & half cream (optional)

1 tablespoon vanilla
few grains salt
1 tablespoon lemon juice
milk to fill freezer (1 gallon)

Mix ingredients in order given. Pour into freezer and finish filling with milk until one or two inches from top. Freeze according to directions for individual freezer. Serves 16.

"Pureed fresh peaches are delicious added to the above recipe."
Erma Jean Crider   *Sanger High School, Sanger*

Strawberry Fluff

1 small pkg. strawberry Jello
  (or other flavor)
1 cup boiling water
2 cups cold orange juice
1 cup dried non-fat milk

1 cup ice-cold water
¼ cup lemon juice
¼ cup sugar
1 pint vanilla or strawberry ice milk or
  ice cream

Dissolve Jello in boiling water. Add orange juice and chill. Mix dry milk with ice cold water and beat to a soft peak. Add lemon juice and beat to a stiff peak. Add sugar and combine chilled gelatin and whipped milk. Serve with a scoop of ice cream on top.* Serves 10.

*Or stir in ice cream and pour into paper cups and freeze for a great pick-me-up snack for the kids.

Sharletta Kay Myers   **Demille Junior High School, Long Beach**

Milk Chocolate Ice Cream

¼ cup sugar
2 tablespoons flour
½ teaspoon salt
3 cups light cream
2 eggs - slightly beaten

2 milk chocolate bars (½ lb. each) broken in
  pieces
1 cup heavy cream
2 teaspoons vanilla

Combine sugar, flour and salt in medium saucepan. Add 1 cup light cream. Cook and stir over medium heat until mixture comes to a boil. Boil and stir 1 minute. Remove from heat, stir small amount of cooked mixture into eggs. Return egg mixture to saucepan and stir until well blended. Add chocolate pieces and stir until melted. Add remainder of cream and vanilla. Blend well. Freeze in ice cream freezer. Makes 3 quarts.

Kitty Worley   **Norte Vista High School, Riverside**

Old-Fashioned Chocolate Ice Cream

2 cups sugar
⅔ cup unsweetened cocoa
¼ cup all-purpose flour
¼ teaspoon salt
2 cups milk

2 eggs, slightly beaten
1 tablespoon vanilla extract
4 cups light cream
1 cup heavy cream

Combine sugar, cocoa, flour and salt in medium saucepan; stir in milk and eggs. Cook and stir over medium heat just until mixture simmers. Remove from heat; blend in vanilla, light cream and heavy cream. Chill. Freeze in ice cream freezer according to manufacturer's directions or freeze in freezer trays until frozen 1-inch in from edges. Turn mixture into large bowl of mixer; beat on high speed 2 minutes. Pour into freezer containers and freeze until firm. About 3 quarts.

Hershey Foods Corporation   **Hershey, Pennsylvania**

Very Quick and Easy Ice Cream

6 large eggs	1 quart half & half
2 cups sugar	2 ½ tablespoons vanilla
1 cup heavy cream	1 ½ to 2 quarts whole milk

Beat eggs until smooth and fluffy, add sugar and beat again; add cream, half & half, and vanilla. Beat again until well mixed. Pour into ice cream freezer. Add whole milk to fill line of freezer. Freeze according to ice cream freezer directions. One pint fruit puree may be substituted for part of the whole milk. Serves 20.

"Use your imagination and add your favorite ingredients. Mexican vanilla makes it extra special."
Sally Pace   **Woodlake High School, Woodlake**

Fried Mexican Ice Cream

1 pint vanilla ice cream	1 egg
½ cup crushed cornflake crumbs or cookie	cooking oil
crumbs	honey
1 teaspoon cinnamon	whipped cream
2 teaspoons sugar	

Scoop 4-5 balls ice cream; shape and freeze. Mix cornflake crumbs, cinnamon and sugar. Roll frozen ice cream balls in half the crumb mixture and freeze again.
Beat egg, dip the coated balls in egg and again in remaining crumbs. Freeze until ready to use.

When ready to serve, heat deep oil to 350°. Place an ice cream ball in a perforated spoon and lower into oil 1 minute. Place in a dessert glass. Drizzle with honey and top with whipped cream. Makes 4-5 servings.

Doris Weimer   **Thousand Oaks High School, Thousand Oaks**

Carole's Sherbet Dessert

1 large tub Cool Whip	½ cup ground nuts
¼ cup sugar	18 coconut macaroons, rolled
pinch of salt	1 pint each of raspberry, lime, orange &
½ teaspoon vanilla	lemon sherbet

Combine Cool Whip, sugar, salt, vanilla, nuts and macaroons and mix well. Pour ½ of the mixture into a buttered 11 x 13" pan. Spread evenly on the bottom of the pan. Spoon onto this all four pints of the sherbet, alternating the flavors to produce a rainbow effect, and smoothing the top. Cover with the other half of the Cool Whip mixture.

Freeze 24 hours, cut into squares and serve. Serves 12.

Kathleen Daudistel   **Hanford High School, Hanford**

Dolly's Delight

1 pkg. (6 ½ oz.) vanilla wafers, crushed
½ cup butter
1 cup confectioner's sugar
2 eggs well beaten
½ cup pecans, chopped

3 pkgs. frozen raspberries, drained
½ cup sugar
½ pint whipping cream
1 tablespoon sugar
1 teaspoon vanilla

Place ½ of the crumbs in an 8 x 12" baking dish. Cream butter and confectioner's sugar until fluffy. Beat eggs and add to cream mixture. Spread this over crumbs. Sprinkle with pecans. Puree berries in blender or mash with masher. Sprinkle berries with sugar. Pour over crumb mixture. Top with whipped cream which has been mixed with 1 tablespoon sugar and 1 teaspoon vanilla. Sprinkle remaining crumbs and pecans on top. Freeze overnight. Take out one hour before serving. Serves 8-12.

Shirley Rusche   *Norte Vista High School, Riverside*

Kathie's Very Favorite Mud Pie

½ pkg. Nabisco chocolate wafers
½ cube butter, melted
½ gallon coffee ice cream

1 ½ cup fudge sauce
whipped cream
slivered almonds

Crush wafers and add butter. Mix well. Press into a 9" pie plate. Cover with soft coffee ice cream. Put into freezer until ice cream is firm. Top with cold fudge sauce (it helps to place it in the freezer for a time to make spreading easier). Store in freezer approximately 10 hours. Top with whipped cream and slivered almonds. Serves 6-8.

"The Chart House special! Keep frozen until serving."
Kathie Baczynski   *Mt. Carmel High School, San Diego*

Peach Cream Torte

¼ pound fresh peaches
4 egg yolks
1 cup granulated sugar
2 teaspoons lemon juice
2 tablespoons Kirsch or Sherry (optional)
1 cup heavy cream, whipped
meringue cookies (recipe below)
¼ cup raspberry jelly, melted (optional)
additional peaches, sliced

Meringue Cookies:
2 egg whites
⅓ cup granulated sugar
¼ cup chopped nuts
1 teaspoon vanilla

Puree in blender enough peaches, unpeeled, to make 1 ¼ cups (about 2 large peaches). Beat egg yolks in top of double boiler. Add peach puree and sugar. Cook, stirring constantly, over simmering water until thickened. Add lemon juice and liquor. Cool. Fold into whipped cream. Pour into an 8" springform pan. Arrange meringue cookies on top and press lightly into mixture. Freeze. To serve, unmold with cookies on bottom and glaze top with raspberry jelly. Slice and serve with fresh sliced peaches, sugared to taste, spooned over each slice. Serves 6 to 8.

Meringue Cookies: Beat whites to soft peaks. Gradually add sugar; beat to stiff peaks. Fold in nuts and vanilla. Drop by tablespoons onto ungreased cookie sheet and bake 1 to 1 ½ hours in a 250° oven.

"Keeps well. Absolutely luscious in the summer-time when the fruit is in season. Not overpoweringly sweet."
Betsy Cosart   **Monache High School, Porterville**

Frozen Fruit Salad

1 6-oz. can orange juice	1 can (2 cups) fruit cocktail and juice
1 6-oz. can lemonade	(3 ounces)
1 small jar maraschino cherries and juice	3 bananas
1 small can crushed pineapple and juice	1 ½ cups 7-Up
(8 ozs)	1 cup water
2 small (10 ounce) boxes fresh strawberries	¼ cup sugar
(2 cups)	

Mix all ingredients together and put into 5-ounce dixie cups. Freeze. Set out and let thaw partially to slush stage before serving. Makes 17 5-oz. cups.
Genevieve Fast   **McLane High School, Fresno**

Instant Party Dessert

1 quart vanilla ice cream	1 bottle Grenadine

Use 8 parfait glasses. Place one scoop of vanilla ice cream in each glass. Add one tablespoon of grenadine. Repeat this order two or three times, depending on the size and shape of your parfait glasses. Place each filled glass on a plate with a doily. Serve a plate of your favorite cookies for an extra touch. Serves 8.

"This dessert may be prepared ahead of time and placed in your freezer. As a precaution, set the parfait glasses on a piece of cardboard so the delicate glasses will not touch ice or cold metal. The cardboard also ensures easy removal."
Mary M. LaVaut   **Jean Farb Middle School, San Diego**

Notes

Fruits & Gelatins

Choco-Bar Fondue

2 8-oz. milk chocolate bars
1 4-oz. semi-sweet chocolate bar
¾ cup light cream

2 to 3 tablespoons kirsch,
   orange-flavored liqueur, or
½ teaspoon almond extract (optional)
Fondue Dippers

Combine chocolate bars and cream in a heavy saucepan; stir constantly over medium-low heat until chocolate is melted. Just before serving, add liqueur or almond extract; pour into fondue pot or chafing dish. Serve warm with a selection of fondue dippers. About 2 ½ cups fondue.

Hershey Foods Corporation　　　　　　　　　　　　　**Hershey, Pennsylvania**

Fruit Kabobs with Sunshine Dip

½ cup sugar
½ cup flour
1 egg, beaten
½ cup canned pineapple juice
½ cup orange juice

2 teaspoons lemon juice
1 pkg. Dream Whip
½ cup milk
4-5 lbs. fruits (variety of colors
   of seasonal fruits)

Stir sugar and flour together in small saucepan. Stir in the beaten egg; gradually stir in fruit juices. Cook over low heat, stirring constantly, until thick. Cool cooked mixture. Prepare Dream Whip according to directions on package. Fold cooled mixture into cream, cover with plastic wrap and refrigerate until serving time.

Wash and dry fruit. Cut fruit into bite-sized pieces (1″ cubes). Thread fruit on 4″ skewers alternating colors. Arrange skewers attractively on a large platter with the dip dish in the center. Put skewers of fruit into a pineapple or grapefruit half and serve the dip on the side. Serves 12.

"Fruit may be prepared ahead and sprinkled with Fruit Fresh or lemon juice to prevent browning. Dip will be good for 6-8 days. Fruit Kabobs also serve as a beautiful, edible centerpiece."
Alice F. Mittermiller　　　　　　　　　　　**La Jolla High School, La Jolla**

24-Hour Salad

2 cups fruit cocktail
2 cups diced pineapple
2 cups Mandarin oranges
2 cups small marshmallows
1 cup whipped unsweetened heavy cream

1 cup sour cream
juice of 1 lemon
1 pkg lemon Jello (thickened but not set)
½ lb. Angelflake coconut or
   ¼ lb. blanched chopped almonds

Drain all fruit well, at least 3 hours. Make Jello, and when thickened, add all ingredients except creams.
Fold in whipped cream and sour cream.

Sheila Dauphin　　　　　　　　　　　**John Glenn High School, Norwalk**

Recipe for "Choco-Bar Fondue" on page 72 →

Chocolate Mint Delight

3 ounces lime Jello (1 small pkg)
1 cup boiling water
2 cups vanilla ice cream (1 pint)

½ teaspoon peppermint extract
½ cup chocolate chips
⅓ cup Cool Whip

Dissolve Jello in boiling water. Add ice cream by spoonfulls and stir until melted. Add peppermint extract and chocolate chips. Chill until set. (About 30 minutes). Garnish with Cool Whip and more chocolate chips. Serves 6.

Mary Tatro   *Clifton Middle School, Monrovia*

Pears Au Chocolat

2 fresh pears
¼ cup sugar
½ cup water

½ teaspoon vanilla
Nut filling (recipe below), optional Creamy
Chocolate Sauce (recipe below)

Core pears from bottom end, but leave stems intact; peel. Slice small amount from bottom of each pear to make a flat base. Combine sugar and water in small saucepan; add pears. Cover, simmer over low heat 15 to 20 minutes (depending on ripeness of pears). Remove from heat add vanilla. Cool pears in syrup. Chill. Serving time: drain pears; spoon in nut filling, if desired. Place in serving dish. Prepare Chocolate Sauce; spoon sauce onto each pear. Pipe with dessert topping or sweetened whipped cream, if desired. Serve additional sauce. 2 servings.

Nut Filling: Combine 3 tablespoons finely chopped nuts, 1 tablespoon confectioner's sugar and ½ teaspoon milk in small bowl until mixture holds together.

Creamy Chocolate Sauce: Combine 3 tablespoons water, 3 tablespoons sugar and 2 tablespoons butter in small saucepan; bring to full boil. Remove from heat; stir in ⅔ cup semi-sweet chocolate Mini Chips. Stir until chocolate has completely melted; beat or whisk until smooth. Cool; about ½ cup sauce.

Hershey Foods Corporation   *Hershey, Pennsylvania*

Bananas Foster

2 tablespoons butter
4 teaspoons brown sugar
2 large bananas

⅛ teaspoon cinnamon
1 ounce rum or brandy
Ice cream

Mix butter and brown sugar in a heavy, shallow skillet and cook over medium heat until caramelized. Cut bananas in half lengthwise and then in thirds crosswise and add to the butter-brown sugar mixture and cook until tender. Add cinnamon. Stir. Add rum or brandy to the top of the mixture. DO NOT STIR. Set aflame with a match and spoon over the individual portions of ice cream while it is still flaming. Serves 6.

"This is a Southern recipe, from the Baton Rouge, Louisiana Junior League cookbook. It is rich enough to sink a battleship . . . I know you'll love it!"

Gwenn Jensen   *Mira Mesa High School, Mira Mesa*

← Recipe for "Pears Au Chocolat" on page 73

Cold Daiquiri Soufflé

10 eggs separated
2 cups sugar
1 cup fresh lime juice
grated rinds of 4 limes
pinch of salt
2 tablespoons unflavored gelatin

½ cup light rum
3 cups heavy cream

Garnish:
Crystallized violets
lime slices
crushed pistachio nuts

Beat egg yolks until light and fluffy. Gradually beat in 1 cup of the sugar until mixture is smooth and lemon-colored. Blend in lime juice, grated rind and salt. Cook and stir over low heat until thickened. Soften gelatin in rum and stir into hot custard to dissolve. Cool. Tie a paper collar around the top of a 6-cup soufflé dish and oil dish and paper. Beat egg whites until foamy, gradually add remaining 1 cup sugar, and beat until peaks form. Fold a large spoonful of custard into egg whites and then fold egg whites into remaining custard. Whip 2 cups of the heavy cream and fold into mixture. Pour into souffle dish and chill thoroughly until set. Whip remaining cream. Remove paper collar and use a pastry bag to decorate top with whipped cream rosettes. Garnish with violets and lime slices. Press nuts gently into sides of soufflé. Serves 12.

Susie Pendleton   *Cerritos High School, Cerritos*

Winnie's Texas Peach Cobbler

Peach Mixture:
2 cups sugar
2 sticks butter
1 teaspoon nutmeg
3 tablespoons flour
1 11-oz. can peach nectar
4 cups sliced large fresh peaches or
    2 #3 cans Alberta peaches

Pie Crust Strips
1 cup Crisco
3 ⅓ cups flour
11 tablespoons cold water
½ stick butter

Peach Mixture: Mix together sugar, butter, nutmeg, flour, and nectar. Boil this mixture for 10 minutes, stirring to blend in flour and keep a smooth consistency. Drain peaches from can and add them to the cooked mixture. Heat for 5 minutes. (When fresh peaches are used, add 1 cup water with the peach nectar.) Pour mixture into an 8 x 11-inch baking dish and cover with pie crust strips.

Pie Crust Strips: Blend Crisco with a small amount of the flour. Add water and mix well. Knead in the remaining flour until the dough is stiff. Roll out the dough on a floured surface. Cut dough into 2-inch by approximately 12-inch strips. Place strips across the pan to cover the cobbler, pinching edges to secure the strips. Melt the butter and brush the pie crust strips thoroughly. Sprinkle the top of the crust lightly with sugar and nutmeg. Bake the cobbler for 50 minutes at 375°. Turn the oven to 400° and bake 10 minutes longer or until well browned.

Serve warm with vanilla ice cream or half and half. Serves 12.

Winnie V. Reed, "World's Greatest Mom"   *Stamford, Texas*

Coeurs 'a La Creme' (Ker ah la Krem)

6-6" squares cheesecloth, moistened
1 8-oz. pkg cream cheese, softened
½ teaspoon vanilla

½ cup powdered sugar, sifted
1 cup whipped cream
1 recipe sauce topping (below)

Line 6 coeur a la creme molds or ½ cup molds with moistened cheesecloth squares, allowing cheesecloth to overhang. In a small mixer bowl blend the cheese and vanilla. Gradually add the sugar, beating at high speed of mixer till light and fluffy. In another bowl beat the whipping cream just until soft peaks form; fold this mixture into the cheese mixture. Spoon the mixture into the molds. Cover and chill several hours or overnight. To serve, invert on plate. Holding onto cheesecloth ends, lift off the mold; peel off the cheesecloth. Serve with Raspberry sauce.

To make Raspberry sauce: In a saucepan combine ½ cup sugar, 1 tablespoon cornstarch and a dash of nutmeg. Mix well. Stir in the juice from one 10 oz. package frozen raspberries, and 2 teaspoons lemon juice. Cook, stirring until thickened. Add the raspberries and cook one minute more, stirring *gently*. Cool and chill until serving time.

"Fancy and Easy!;"
Gloria Reece   *Porterville High School, Porterville*

Cherry Torte

1 cup all-purpose flour
5 tablespoons confectioner's sugar
½ cup soft butter or margarine
2 eggs
1 ½ cup granulated sugar
½ teaspoon salt
⅓ cup all purpose flour
¼ teaspoon baking powder
1 teaspoon vanilla

¾ chopped walnuts
1 1-lb. can pitted, red tart cherries, drained

Topping:
1 pint heavy cream, whipped
½ cup water
cherry juice
½ cup granulated sugar
2 tablespoons cornstarch
few drops red food coloring

Mix 1 cup flour, confectioner's sugar and butter. Pat in the bottom of an 8 x 13" pan. Bake at 350° (325° if using glass pan) for about 15 minutes or until lightly browned. Cool. Beat eggs with granulated sugar until thick and frothy. Add salt, ¼ cup flour, baking powder and vanilla. Beat well. Fold in nuts and cherries. Pour over baked crust. Bake for 40 minutes longer at 325°F. Cool. Add topping just before serving.

Topping directions: Spread whipped cream over torte in swirls. Combine water, cherry juice, sugar and cornstarch. Cook, stirring constantly, until thickened and clear. Add red food coloring as desired. Spoon warm sauce over individual servings. Serves 12.

"Not expensive or difficult, but very elegant!"
Mrs. Lois Armstrong   *Sonora High School, La Habra*

Banana Split Dessert

1 stick margarine
2 cups graham cracker crumbs
2 cups powdered sugar
2 sticks margarine
2 eggs
4 sliced bananas

2 cups crushed pineapple, drained
2 pints frozen strawberries
9 oz. Cool Whip
¼ cup chopped walnuts
12 maraschino cherries

Melt margarine and stir graham cracker crumbs. Line the bottom of a 9 x 12 x 2" baking pan with crumb mixture. Bake crust at 350°F. for 5 minutes. Chill. Combine 2 cups powdered sugar, 2 sticks margarine and 2 eggs; whip until creamy. Spread on top of crust and chill. Layer the banana slices on top of the sugar mixture. Then layer the pineapple on top of the bananas, then the strawberries on top of the pineapple. Stir and spread the Cool Whip on top. Sprinkle top with nuts. Garnish with cherries. Chill at least one hour before serving. Serves 12.

Clara Bartlett   **John W. North High School, Riverside**

Sunshine Salad

1 cup boiling water
1 3-oz. pkg. lemon-flavored gelatin
½ cup cold water

½ teaspoon salt
1 can crushed pineapple
½ cup shredded carrots

Topping for Sunshine Salad:

1 small carton of whipped cream
1 3-oz. pkg lemon-flavored gelatin

Pour boiling water over gelatin in bowl. Stir until gelatin is dissolved. Stir in *cold water*, salt and pineapple (with syrup). Chill until slightly thickened but not set. Stir in carrots. Pour into a 4-cup ring mold or into 6 individual molds. Chill until firm.

Mix whipped cream until fluffy and add gelatin. Spread over gelatin after removing from the mold. Serves 6.

Priscilla Robinson   **Mt. View High School, El Monte**

Peaches and Cream

1 box Coconut Pecan frosting mix
1 box yellow cake mix
2 eggs
½ cup butter or margarine (melted)

Topping:
1 pound sour cream
1 egg
1 can sliced peaches (drained)
1 pound 14 ounces

Mix together the first 4 ingredients until cake mix is moistened. Press into an ungreased 8 x 13" or 9 x 11" pan. Bake at 350°F. for 10-15 minutes or until toothpick comes out clean. Blend sour cream with the egg. Place drained peaches over cake and pour sour cream mixture over the peaches. Bake at 325°F until the sour cream cracks.

Marcy Bergner   **Kearny High School, San Diego**

Cherry Dessert

1 large can cherry pie filling
1 large can of crushed pineapple, undrained
1 pkg. yellow cake mix
1 cup pecans, coarsely cut
1 cup coconut
½ cup butter or margarine

Butter a 9 x 13″ pan, spread cherries in bottom, cover with pineapple and sprinkle dry cake mix over top of fruit. Sprinkle nuts and coconut over top and dot with ½ cup butter or margarine, (or melt and drizzle over top). Bake one hour at 350°F. or 1 hour and 10 minutes at 325°F. Serve with topping, whipped cream or ice cream. Serves 12.

Karen Iverson   *Sierra Vista Jr High School, La Puente*

Lisa's Cherry Treats

2 8-oz. pkgs. cream cheese
1 tablespoon lemon juice
¾ cup sugar
2 eggs
1 teaspoon vanilla
vanilla wafers
muffin liners
cherry pie filling

Mix first 5 ingredients together well. Line each muffin cup with a paper liner in which a vanilla wafer is placed. Fill each cup almost to the top and bake at 325-350° until tops crack slightly or they barely brown. Top with pie filling. Serves 12-14.

Elaine Humphries   *Memorial Junior High School, San Diego*

Fruit Delight

1 ½ cup frozen raspberries, defrosted
1 ½ cup fresh strawberry slices
3 to 4 tablespoons Grand Marnier
6 fresh peach halves
  (canned may be substituted)
1 quart vanilla ice cream
whipped cream
whole strawberries for garnish
Pirouettes (curled cookies) for garnish

Thaw and crush raspberries. Blend them with strawberries and Grand Marnier. Place peach half in parfait glass. Then a scoop of ice cream, fruit mixture, whipped cream. Garnish with whole strawberry and pirouettes. Serve immediately. Serves 6. Use 6 parfait glasses.

Jeri Lentz   *Grossmont High School, La Mesa*

Jello Chiffon

1 4-oz. pkg Jello (any flavor)
1 4-oz. carton Cool Whip

Follow directions on Jello package. In four parfait glasses equally divide half of Jello into glasses. Refrigerate the rest of the Jello and the parfait glasses of Jello. When Jello has thickened fold in Cool Whip. Divide equally in parfait glasses. Refrigerate at least 2 hours before serving. Serves 4.

"Fruit can be added to Jello if desired."
Carol Krause   *Alta Loma Jr High School, Alta Loma*

Fruit Cobbler

2-3 cups fresh fruit
1 cup flour
1 cup sugar
½ teaspoon salt

2 teaspoons baking powder
¼ cup shortening or margarine
1 egg

Grease a 9″ round pan and arrange 2-3 cups of fresh fruit in the pan. Sift dry ingredients together. Cut in shortening (or butter). Add egg until entire mixture is crumbly. Sprinkle dry mixture over top of fresh fruit. Bake at 350° until golden brown (about 20-30 minutes). Serves 4-6

"This can be frozen ahead of time and slightly thawed before serving. (Be sure center is well done before removing from oven). Mixture can be doubled and put in a 9 x 13″ pan. Increase baking time."
Denise Hammond   **Yuba City High School, Yuba City**

Rhubarb Crunch

6 cups rhubarb (fresh or frozen)
2 cups sugar
¼ cup orange juice concentrate
2 tablespoons flour
½ teaspoon pumpkin pie spice

Topping:
1 cup flour
1 cup sugar
1 egg
½ teaspoon salt
1 teaspoon baking powder

Combine rhubarb, 2 cups sugar, orange juice concentrate, 2 tablespoons flour, and pumpkin pie spice. Put in a 9 x 13″ greased pan.

Combine 1 cup flour, 1 cup sugar, egg, salt, and baking powder. Sprinkle on top of rhubarb. Bake at 350° oven 45 minutes to an hour until rhubarb is tender and topping is light brown. Serve warm or cold with whipped cream or ice cream. Serves 8-10. Absolutely delicious!
Sharon Kleven   **San Gabriel High School, San Gabriel**

Apple Crisp

6-8 apples (green are best)
¼ cup water
1 teaspoon cinnamon
nutmeg to taste

Topping:
¾ cup flour
½ cup sugar
½ cup brown sugar
⅓ cup butter or margarine

Pare, core and slice apples into a long glass pan. Sprinkle apples with water, cinnamon and nutmeg. Mix topping ingredients with pastry blender and crumble over the apples. Bake 30-45 minutes at 325°F. Serves 8-10.

"An old family favorite — good for winter nights by a fire!"
Marge Dieterich   **West Covina High School, West Covina**

Blueberry, Apple or Cherry Squares

1 cup sugar
2 cubes butter or margarine
3 cups flour

1 egg yolk
2 cans pie filling of your choice

Butter a 13 x 9″ dish. Set aside. Blend sugar and butter; cut in flour. Add egg yolk and mix. Pat ½ of crust mixture into pan. Spread 2 cans of filling over crust. Sprinkle remainder of crust on top of filling. Bake at 400°F. for 30 minutes. Serve warm with or without ice cream. Serves 9-12.

"Takes 10 minutes to assemble. Keep 2 cans of pie filling in the cupboard and you'll always have a quick and delicious last minute dessert. Great for potlucks too!"
Linda Hsieh   **Alhambra High School, Alhambra**

Red Raspberry Russian Cream

½ pint (1 cup) whipping cream
¾ cup granulated sugar
1 envelope unflavored gelatin
¾ cup cold water

1 cup commercial sour cream
1 teaspoon vanilla
1 pkg frozen raspberries or strawberries

Warm whipping cream and sugar in a double boiler until lukewarm. Soak gelatin in the ¾ cup cold water 5 minutes; add to cream and continue to heat until hot. When gelatin and sugar have completely dissolved, remove from heat and cool. When mixture begins to thicken, stir in sour cream. Beat entire mixture until smooth; add flavoring and pour into individual molds or pyrex cups. Let set in refrigerator about 4 hours or until firm.

To unmold: Lower mold almost to rim, in bowl of warm water for 10 seconds (if mold is glass, use hot water); remove. Gently loosen gelatin with paring knife. If it's not easy to loosen after one dipping, repeat. Then place chilled serving dish upside down, on top of mold; invert. Carefully lift off mold, leaving dessert on dish. Top with thawed berries. Serves 6-8.

Audrey Hallett   **Hoover High School, San Diego**

Mrs. "B's"

½ cup butter
2 cups powdered sugar
2 eggs
½ teaspoon almond extract

½ teaspoon lemon extract
1 small flat can crushed pineapple
½ pint whipping cream
½ lb. vanilla wafers

Cream butter and sugar. Add beaten eggs, beating well after each egg. Add extracts. Drain pineapple. Whip cream; *do not add sugar.* Crush wafers. Arrange wafers on the bottom of dish. Add egg mixtures for first layer. Add drained pineapple as second layer. Add whipped cream as third layer and crushed wafers as last layer. Serves 10.

"Very rich but delicious!!"
Gage Jones   **South Pasadena High School, South Pasadena**

Sprinkle Dessert

4 cups rhubarb or any fresh fruit
1 6-oz. pkg. raspberry Jello
1 cup sugar
1 cup water

1 box yellow cake mix
½ cup coconut
½ cup nuts
1½ cups margarine

Sprinkle ingredients in the order given into a 9 x 13 inch pan. Slice margarine thinly and place on top of cake mix. Bake in 350° oven for 35 minutes. Serves 18.

"When cooled, place in refrigerator. Keep in refrigerator until it is finished."
Antoinette De Neve   *Jones Junior High School, Baldwin Park*

Mexican Banana Casserole

1 pkg. cream cheese
¼ cup packed brown sugar
¼ cup rum
3 tablespoons half & half

⅛ teaspoon cinnamon
5 bananas
1 tablespoon butter

Cream the cheese, brown sugar, rum, half & half and cinnamon in the blender. Cover and blend on high speed until smooth. Slice the bananas. Put half on the bottom of a greased, 1-quart casserole. Spread with half the mixture; dot with butter. Add the remaining bananas, spread with remaining mixture. Bake uncovered at 325° until hot and bubbly 20 to 25 minutes. Can be topped with whipped cream when served.

"Easy & Fast!"
Karen Blue   *Roosevelt Junior High School, Glendale*

Wild Raspberry Dessert

2 cubes butter
2 tablespoons sugar
1 ½ cups flour
1 cube margarine
2 3-oz. pkgs. cream cheese
2 cups powdered sugar

1 cup chopped nuts
1 cup boiling water
2 3-oz. pkgs. wild raspberry Jello
2 pkgs. frozen raspberries
Cool Whip

Mix together butter, sugar and flour. Spread this mixture into a 9 x 13-inch pan. Bake at 350° until golden brown, approximately 15 minutes. Cool after removing from the oven. Mix margarine, cream cheese, and powdered sugar. Spread mixture on top of cooled baked crust. Sprinkle chopped nuts over the cream cheese mixture. Mix the two packages of Jello with one cup boiling water. Add raspberries and their juice to the Jello. Cool mixture until it is partially set. Spoon the Jello mixture on top of the layer of nuts. Spread cool whip over the entire dessert. Chill until it is ready to serve.

"This recipe was given to me about ten years ago by a very dear friend, Kit Lane Warren, from Edison High School. Each time it is served, the compliments continue."
Gerry Henderson   *Temple City High School, Temple City*

Pink Flamingo

2 8-oz. pkgs cream cheese
2 cups Eagle brand milk
⅔ cup lemon juice
2 teaspoons vanilla

1 teaspoon red food coloring
Vanilla wafers
2-3 bananas
½ pint whipping cream

Soften cream cheese; beat until fluffy. Add milk, lemon juice, vanilla and red food coloring. Mix well and pour into a vanilla wafer crust in a 9 x 13″ dish. Slice bananas over the top. Spread whipped cream over the top. Chill and serve.

Sherril Stubblefield   **Judkins Intermediate School, Pismo Beach**

Fruit Fluff

1 13-oz. can evaporated milk
1 3-oz. pkg Jello
½ cup sugar
¾ cup boiling water

1 lemon or orange
1 cup chopped fresh fruit
12 graham crackers

Pour evaporated milk into large mixing bowl and place in freezer to chill until ice crystals form on top. In a separate small mixing bowl, dissolve Jello and sugar in boiling water. Let stand until cool, but not thickened. Whip chilled milk with electric mixer until it is light and fluffy. Beat in grated rind and juice of a lemon or an orange. Fold in Jello mixture. Stir in 1 cup of any chopped fresh fruit. Roll out graham crackers in plastic bag to make crumbs. Place ½ of the crumbs on bottom of rectangular cake pan (13 x 9 x 2″). Pour in fluff mixture. Sprinkle rest of crumbs on top and chill well in refrigerator. Cut into squares when ready to serve. Makes 12 to 15 servings.

"To reduce calories: Use D-Zerta (low-cal gelatin) in place of Jello, and Skim evaporated milk."
Sydney Fox   **Orange Glen High School, Escondido**

Citronfromage (Lemon Fluff)

6 eggs (separated)
2 cups sugar
2 envelopes unflavored gelatin (Knox)
juice of 2 lemons
    (+ 2 teaspoons grated rind, optional)

juice of 2 oranges
    (+ 2 teaspoons rind, optional)
1 pint whipping cream, whipped

In a large four-quart mixing bowl, beat egg yolks and sugar until lemon colored. Soak gelatin in one cup cold water and melt over hot water or in the microwave oven. Add gelatin and the juice from the lemons and oranges to the egg yolk mixture. Beat. Chill until the mixture begins to thicken. Beat stiffly beaten egg whites and the whipped cream into the egg yolk mixture. Fold in grated rinds, if desired. Chill until set. Serve topped with additional whipped cream. Serves 12.

"This recipe makes a light dessert which is perfect to serve after a dinner meal. It is a Danish recipe. The gelatin can be dissolved quickly in a microwave oven."
Judith Lindsay   **Lewis Junior High School, San Diego**

Strawberry Yummo

2 10-oz. pkgs of frozen strawberries
1 cup water
½ cup sugar
2 teaspoons lemon juice
4 teaspoons cornstarch
1¼ cup cold water

50 large marshmallows
1 cup milk
2 pkgs Dream Whip
1¼ cup graham cracker crumbs
¼ cup chopped nuts
¼ cup melted butter

Heat strawberries with cup of water, sugar and lemon juice. Dissolve cornstarch in 1¼ cups cold water. Stir into strawberries, cook until thick and clear. Cool. Melt marshmallows and milk over low heat, cool thoroughly. Make Dream Whip — *no vanilla*. Fold Dream Whip into marshmallow mixture. Mix graham cracker crumbs, nuts and margarine and press into a 9 x 13" pan. Spread marshmallow mixture over crust. Spread strawberry mixture over that. Refrigerate until firm. Garnish with Cool Whip if desired. Serves 12-15.

Shirley Rice   *Bakersfield High School, Bakersfield*

Raspberry Jello Delight

large pkg. raspberry Jello
2 cups boiling water
1 cup cold water
1 cup applesauce

3-4 cups frozen raspberries
medium carton sour cream
1 ½ cups miniature marshmallows

Combine Jello with boiling water, dissolve completely. Add cold water, applesauce, and frozen raspberries together. Stir and set in refrigerator. Combine sour cream and marshmallows. Spread on top of set Jello. Let this set overnight for best results. Serves 16.

"Additional serving suggestion — Serve on angel food cake."
Faye Nielsen   *Rosemead High School, Rosemead*

Rhonda's Almond Jello

2 pkgs. unflavored Jello
1 ¾ cups cold water
6 tablespoons granulated sugar
1 ½ cups milk
1 tablespoon almond extract
1 16-oz. can fruit cocktail*

*Variation:
1 16-oz. can of lichee nuts
1 6½-oz. can mandarin oranges and
    10-12 fresh strawberries

In a large bowl, dissolve gelatin and ½ cup cold water with the sugar. Stir until well mixed. Bring rest of water (1 ¼ cup) to a boil and pour over gelatin mixture. Stir until mixture is clear. Add milk and almond extract. Pour into a 7 ½" x 12" pan. Refrigerate until set. Chill fruits. When ready to serve, cut almond Jello into ¾-inch squares. Lift carefully into individual dessert glasses. Garnish with chilled fruits and pour some syrup from canned fruits over almond Jello. Serves 9.

Brenda Wong   *Yuba Gardens School, Olive Hurst*

Lime Delight

1 13-oz can evaporated milk
1 small package lime Jello
1 ⅓ cup hot water
¼ cup lime juice
2 teaspoons lemon juice

1 cup sugar
green food coloring
2 cups or 1 pkg chocolate wafers
⅓ cup melted butter

Chill canned milk until icy but not frozen. Dissolve Jello in hot water and chill until partially set. Whip Jello until fluffy. Stir in juices and sugar. Whip canned milk into peaks. Fold two mixtures together. Add green food coloring.

Crust: Combine cookies and butter. Press into the bottom of a 13 x 9 x 2" pan. Pour Jello mixture into pan over crust. Sprinkle crushed wafers over the top.

"A nice summer dessert. Also very nice complement to a holiday meal at Christmas time!"
Joretta Stewart   **Olive Junior High School, Baldwin Park**

Jello Delight

1 small box Jello (lime),
  but you can use any flavor
¾ cup hot water

¾ cold water
1 small carton of yogurt (lime),
  but you can use any flavor

Empty box of Jello into mixing bowl. Dissolve with ¾ cup hot water. Add ¾ cup cold water and mix well. Add carton of yogurt. Beat with electric mixer until frothy. Pour into bowls (4 small dessert dishes). Let set until set or overnight. Garnish with whipped cream.

"The same flavor of Jello should be used with the same flavor of yogurt, but feel free to experiment!"
Susan Schulte   **Notre Dame High School, Riverside**

Orange Cooler

1 pint Cool Whip
1 pint cottage cheese

1 3-oz. pkg. orange Jello
1 can mandarin oranges, drained

Place all ingredients in a bowl, and mix well. Place in serving dishes or refrigerator bowl and refrigerate at least 1 hour. Serve. Makes 8 servings.
Shirley Rusche   **Norte Vista High School, Riverside**

Yogurt Snow

2 egg whites
8 oz. apricot yogurt

8 oz. grapes, halved and seeded

Whisk the egg whites until stiff and fold in the yogurt. Layer the yogurt and grapes into tall glass dishes. Top with grapes. Serves 4-6.
Nan McCoull   **Grant Middle School, Escondido**

Peach Cobbler

3 cups sliced peaches
¾ cup sugar
4 tablespoons butter or margarine
½ cup milk
1 cup flour

1 teaspoon baking powder
½ teaspoon salt
1 cup sugar
1 tablespoon cornstarch or 2 of flour
¼ teaspoon salt

Butter sides of 9 x 6 x 2 ½" baking dish and add sliced peaches. Cream together ¾ cup sugar, butter, milk, 1 cup flour, 1 teaspoon baking powder, and ½ teaspoon salt to make batter. Spread batter over peaches. Sift together 1 cup sugar, 1 tablespoon constarch, and ¼ teaspoon salt. Sprinkle over batter and pour 1 cup boiling water over all and bake 50 to 60 minutes at 325°F. Serve with cream or ice cream. Serves 6.

"A good Southern dish!"
Alcyone Bass   **Hamilton Junior High School, Long Beach**

Fried Apple Slices

½ cup sugar
1 teaspoon cinnamon

6 apples
6 tablespoons butter or margarine

Mix sugar and cinnamon together in a small bowl. Wash, core, and slice apples. Melt butter or margarine in a skillet. Arrange apple slices in skillet and cook for about five minutes. Turn slices over and cook five more minutes. Remove apple slices from skillet and coat one at a time in cinnamon-sugar mixture. (Be sure to coat both sides). Serve warm. Makes 6 servings.

Linda Robinson   **Sinaloa Junior High School, Simi Valley**

Chocolate Fondue

12 oz. chocolate chips
¼ cup cointreau or triple sec

2 cans sweetened condensed milk

Melt ingredients together over low heat - take care chocolate doesn't burn. Cut fruits to dip - tangerines, bananas, strawberries, etc. Serves 10.

Melinda Mang   **Laguna Beach High School, Laguna Beach**

Lemon Fluff

1 can evaporated milk (large)
1 pkg. lemon Jello (small size)
1 ¾ cup hot water

¼ cup lemon juice
1 cup sugar
2 ½ cups wafer crumbs

Chill milk until icy cold. Dissolve Jello in hot water. Chill Jello mixture until partially set. Whip until light and fluffy. Add lemon juice and sugar. Whip the cold milk thoroughly. Fold milk into Jello mixture. Line a 9 x 13" pan with vanilla wafer crumbs. Pour lemon fluff over crumbs and top with more crumbs. Chill. Serves 12.

"Simple to make ahead of time."
Mildred Chandler   **Joe Walker Junior High School, Quartz Hill**

Meringues

Meringue Shells

2 egg whites
⅛ teaspoon cream of tartar
¼ teaspoon salt

1 teaspoon vanilla
⅔ cup sugar

Heat oven to 275°F. Line a cookie sheet with brown paper. In a small bowl, beat egg whites, cream of tartar, salt and vanilla until frothy. Gradually add sugar, beating continuously until stiff peaks form. Do not underbeat. Using 2 heaping teaspoonfuls for each shell, spoon onto prepared pan. Make a deep well in the center of each, spreading meringues into 3" circles. Bake at 275° about 1 hour or until crisp and very lightly browned. Turn oven off; leave in oven with door closed 1 ½ hours. Remove from oven. Cool completely. Serves 8.

"For best results, freeze bowl and beaters before using. TIP: Fill with ice cream fresh fruit, prepared fruit filling, or custard. 70 calories each."
Ann Clark, Courtesy of Vivian Giarratano   **Pt. Loma High School, San Diego**

Baked Alaska

1 quart ice cream
1 baked 9" cake layer
6 egg whites

¾ cup sugar
½ teaspoon cream of tartar

Day before or very early:

Pack softened ice cream into a bowl not larger than 8" in diameter. Freeze until very firm. Bake 9" layer.

Day of serving:

Cover a stiff cardboard circle, several inches larger than the cake layer, with aluminum foil. (This is both baking utensil and server). Place cake on foil server.

Make meringue:

Beat egg whites until foamy; gradually add sugar and cream of tartar, beating after each addition; beat until sugar is dissolved and meringue stands in stiff, glossy peaks. Unmold ice cream onto cake layer, centering it carefully. Completely cover ice cream and cake with meringue. Place in 450° (very hot) oven until delicately browned, about 5 minutes. Serve immediately.

You may prepare this a day ahead, totally, except for the browning. That you do just before serving. Serves 8-20.

"OR cut a 15 x 10" cake into 3 long strips. Spread 1 quart softened ice cream between strips. Wrap in aluminum foil and freeze until ice cream is firm. Just before serving, unwrap and place on foil-lined board or baking sheet. Cover top and sides and ends with meringue. Bake at 500° for 3 to 5 minutes, or until lightly browned. Serve immediately."

Sue Walters   **Horace Mann Junior High School, San Diego**

Red-Letter Day Torte

Crust:
2 cups flour
1 teaspoon salt
1 cup shortening
1 egg

Meringue:
3 egg whites
1 teaspoon vanilla
¼ teaspoon cream of tartar
dash salt
¾ cup sugar
1 cup walnuts
nutmeg

Filling:
¾ cup sugar
3 slightly beaten egg yolks
3 tablespoons quick-cooking tapioca
¼ teaspoon red food coloring
*1-lb. can pitted red cherries (water-packed)
*reserve juice — add water to juice to make
1 cup — reserve cherries

Sift flour and salt and cut in shortening. Add slightly beaten egg. Stir until a soft dough forms. Pat over bottom of a 11 ½ x 7 ½ x 1 ½" baking pan. Bake at 425°F for 20 minutes. Add all filling ingredients together except cherries. Let stand 5 minutes. Cook and stir until mixture thickens and comes to a boil. Add cherries and 2 teaspoons lemon juice. Cool slightly.

Meringue: Beat whites with vanilla and cream of tartar, and dash of salt until soft peaks form. Slowly add sugar, beating until stiff peaks form. Fold in walnuts. Pour filling over baked crust; top with meringue. Sprinkle with nutmeg. Bake at 350°F for about 20 minutes or until lightly brown. Cool, cut into squares. Serves 9-12.

"Best if eaten the same day so meringue doesn't pull away from sides."
Roberta Baker   **Fontana High School, Fontana**

Lemon Angel Torte

4 eggs, separated
¼ teaspoon cream of tartar
¼ teaspoon salt
¾ cup sugar

Filling:
¾ cup granulated sugar
½ cup lemon juice
2 tablespoons grated lemon rind
dash of salt
2 cups whipping cream

Preheat oven to 450°. Beat together until frothy 4 egg whites, ¼ teaspoon cream of tartar and salt. Gradually beat in ¾ cup sugar in middle of bowl (don't let any sugar get on bowl). Beat to very stiff peaks, about 7 minutes. Spread in *well-buttered* 10" pie plate. Place in preheated oven; *turn-off heat*. Let shell stand in closed oven 5 hours or overnight. *Don't peek!!*

Beat egg yolks in small bowl until thick and lemon colored. Gradually beat in ¾ cup sugar, lemon juice, peel and dash of salt. Cook and stir over gently boiling water until thick, about 8 minutes; cover; cool. Whip cream. Fold half into cooled lemon filling. Spoon filling into shell, then rest of whipped cream covering entire filling, including edges. Chill at least 5 hours or overnight. Pie may also be frozen.

Jeri Lentz   **Grossmont High School, La Mesa**

Swedish Meringue Torte

3 egg whites
⅛ teaspoon cream of tartar
⅛ teaspoon salt
grated lemon rind

½ cup plus 2 tablespoons sugar
¼ cup ground almonds
⅓ cup sifted cornstarch
*Fillings (recipes below)

Combine egg whites, cream of tartar, salt and lemon rind in large bowl. Beat until soft peaks form. Blend in ½ cup sugar one tablespoon at a time. Continue beating until very thick and dull. Combine the remaining 2 tablespoons sugar and remaining ingredients. Sift into the meringue and fold in quickly.

Line 2 cookie sheets with foil. Mark out one 9″ circle on each cookie sheet with a pencil. Spread or pipe the meringue mixture evenly over the circles. Bake at 225-250° until crisp and dry but still white (about 40 minutes). Cool and peel off carefully. Serves 4.

*Fillings:

Strawberry Filling
1 cup sliced sweetened strawberries, drained
1-2 cups whipping cream, whipped

1 tablespoon kirsch, cognac, or Cointreau
  (optional)
¼ cup almonds, halved

Combine strawberries and ⅔ of whipping cream. Blend in liqueur. Spread on one meringue layer. Cover with other meringue layer. Top with remaining whipping cream, preferably in an ornate design of swirls and rosettes. Stud whipped cream topping with almonds. Chill tart before serving.

Chocolate Filling:
½ pkg dark sweet chocolate pudding,
  made with half milk, half cream

½ cup heavy cream, whipped
½ cup toasted almonds, halved

Cook chocolate pudding according to directions. Chill. Fold in ¼ cup whipped cream. Spread pudding between meringue layers. Cover top layer and side of cake with remaining whipped cream, tracing decorative swirls. Stud top and side of cake with toasted almond halves. Chill before serving.

*A meringue tart with chocolate filling is sometimes called a "Rolla Tarta".
Sue Hope   **Lompoc Valley Middle School, Lompoc**

Sandra's Meringue Delight!

18 individual soda crackers
4 egg whites
1 cup sugar

1 teaspoon vanilla
1 cup chopped walnuts
sliced strawberries or other fresh fruit

Grease square pan lightly. Roll soda crackers out fine. Beat egg whites until stiff peaks form, adding sugar as you beat. Fold in vanilla, chopped nuts and cracker crumbs. Put into cake pan and bake at 350°F for 25-30 minutes. Cool. Serve with whipped cream and sliced strawberries or other fruit. Serves 8.

"Should not be made more than 1 day in advance."
Sandra French   **Long Beach Unified School District, Long Beach**

Pineapple Meringue Cake

1 cup sifted flour
2 teaspoons baking powder
⅛ teaspoon salt
4 large eggs, separated
1 ½ cup sugar
2 teaspoons vanilla
½ cup shortening
5 tablespoons milk
¾ cup finely chopped nuts (walnuts or
    pecans)

Pineapple Filling:
1 3½-oz. can crushed pineapple
1 cup whipping cream
1 ½ teaspoons powdered sugar
¼ teaspoon vanilla

Resift flour with baking powder and salt. Set aside. Beat egg whites to soft peaks; gradually beat in 1 cup sugar, continuing to beat until stiff. Fold in 1 teaspoon vanilla. Set aside. Cream shortening with remaining ½ cup sugar. Blend in flour mixture alternately with milk. Stir in remaining teaspoon vanilla. Divide batter between 2 greased and floured 8″ cake pans. Top each with half the meringue and sprinkle with nuts. Bake at 350°F for 40 minutes or until tests done. Remove from oven and cool in pans. Loosen edges of cake and meringue and turn out. Place one layer meringue side down on serving plate. Spread with pineapple filling. Top with second layer, meringue side down on serving place. Spread with pineapple filling. Top with second layer, meringue side up. Refrigerate at least several hours before serving.

Pineapple Filling: Drain pineapple. Beat cream with sugar and vanilla until stiff. Fold in drained pineapple. Serves 10.

"Light and luscious!"
Nanci Burkhart   *Hueneme High School, Oxnard*

Brownie A La Alaska

1 block uncut brownie
brick of ice cream
5 egg whites
⅛ teaspoon salt

½ cup sugar
2 teaspoons instant coffee
¼ teaspoon vanilla
shaved chocolate (optional)

Place brownie on breadboard or baking sheet covered with heavy brown paper. Beat egg whites with salt, until soft peaks form. Add sugar, 1 tablespoon at a time, beating constantly. Beat in coffee and vanilla; continue beating until mixture will hold its shape. Center ice cream brick on brownie; cover completely with meringue. Bake at 425°F for 5 to 6 minutes, until delicately brown. Top with shaved chocolate, if desired. Serve immediately. Serves 6.

Andrea Roberts   *Apple Valley Jr. High School, Apple Valley*

Pavlova

4 egg whites
2 cups sugar

1 teaspoon white vinegar
1 teaspoon cornstarch

Beat egg whites. Fold sugar into the egg whites. Carefully add vinegar and cornstarch to this mixture. Place meringue in a mound on a pie plate. Be sure meringue is 1" from the edge of the plate. Bake in an oven set at 250° for 1 to 1 ½ hours or until meringue is light brown and hard to the touch. Top with fresh fruit mixed in whipped cream and serve.

Sue Zallar   ***Capistrano Valley High School, Mission Viejo***

Pies &
Pastries

Apple Pie and Crust

½ cup sugar
3 tablespoons flour
¼ teaspoon nutmeg
¼ teaspoon cinnamon
dash salt
5 cups thinly sliced pared tart apples
½ - ¾ cup apple juice
1 tablespoon butter or margarine

Pastry:
1 cup + 2 tablespoons Gold Medal flour
½ teaspoon salt
⅓ cup salad oil
2 to 3 tablespoons cold water

Heat oven to 425°F. Prepare pastry (flour, salt, salad oil and water). Put in pie pan. Stir together sugar, flour, nutmeg, cinnamon and salt; mix with apples and juice. Turn into pastry-lined pie pan; dot with butter. Cover with top crush which has slits cut in it; seal and flute. Cover edge with 2-3 inches of aluminum foil to prevent excessive browning; remove foil last 15 minutes of baking. Bake 40-50 minutes or until crust is brown and juice begins to bubble through slits in crust.

Betty M. Williams   *East Bakersfield High School, Bakersfield*

Quickie Cream Cheese Pie

⅓ cup butter or margarine
¼ cup sugar
1 ½ cups graham cracker crumbs
    (about 18 crackers)

1 8-oz. pkg. cream cheese,
    room temperature
1 ⅓ cups half and half
1 3 ¼-oz. package instant vanilla pudding

Melt butter or margarine in a 9″ glass pie plate in the microwave about 45 seconds on high power. Mix in sugar and crumbs. Press crumb mixture evenly over pie plate, bottom and sides. Bake in microwave oven for 2 minutes on high power, rotating plate halfway through baking period. Cool crust quickly in freezer.

Blend cream cheese until smooth; gradually beat in half and half. Add pudding mix and beat quickly until smooth*. Pour into cooled crumb crust and chill. Serve plain, with fruit or your favorite canned fruit pie filling. Serves 8.

*Once you add the vanilla pudding the mixture sets almost immediately!!

"It's easy and delicious! Bad news — approximately 365 calories per plain serving and 455 calories with cherry pie filling!!"
Sharon D. Jenkins   *Perris Valley Jr. High School, Perris*

Chess Pie

3 whole eggs, beaten slightly
1 ¾ cup sugar
¼ pound butter, melted
2 teaspoons flour

2 teaspoons corn meal, scant
1 teaspoon vanilla
1 teaspoon lemon flavoring, optional

Combine all ingredients and pour into unbaked pie shell. Cook 325°F for about 1 hour or until it won't shake. Serves 6.

"Very rich. I like it best without the lemon. Was called Chess Pie because you could pick it up with your fingers and eat while playing chess. Very Southern, y'all!"
Alcyone Bass   *Hamilton Jr. High School, Long Beach*

Two-Crust Lemon Pie

Pastry:
2 cups sifted flour
1 teaspoon salt
⅔ cup shortening
5 to 7 tablespoons cold water

Topping:
1 egg white
1 tablespoon sugar
¼ teaspoon cinnamon

Filling:
⅓ cup flour
1 ¼ cups sugar
¾ cup butter or margarine
3 eggs
⅓ cup water
⅓ cup lemon juice
2 teaspoons grated lemon rind

Pastry: Sift flour and salt together into a bowl. Cut in shortening with a pastry blender until pieces are the size of small peas. Add water, one tablespoon at a time, until mixture is moistened. Form into a ball and roll pie crust size.

Filling: Cream together flour, sugar and butter until light and creamy. Add eggs and beat until light and fluffy. Combine the last three ingredients and stir into creamed ingredients, mixing thoroughly. Pour filling into unbaked pastry-lined pie tin. Place top crust over filling and fold up the bottom crust over the top and crimp the edges. Brush top crust with egg white. Combine 1 tablespoon sugar and ¼ teaspoon cinnamon and sprinkle over the top crust. Remember to cut air vents in top crust. Bake in moderate oven (350°F) for 50 minutes. Crust should be golden brown and blistered. Knife inserted into filling should come out clean and clear like a custard or pumpkin pie. Serves 6.

"Pie can be frozen unbaked — and should be completely thawed to bake after being frozen. Follow recipe directions."
Marie Humphrey   *Grant School, Escondido*

Ice Cream Chocolate Pie

1 cup milk
1 3¾-ounce box chocolate instant pudding
1 pint vanilla ice cream

1 baked pie shell
Whipped cream and chocolate shavings
*   for topping*

Beat milk and pudding together and then beat in ice cream a little at a time. Pour into baked pie shell. Chill for one hour or more in refrigerator. Top with whipped cream or whip cream substitute and garnish with chocolate shavings. Serves 6.

Erma Jean Crider   *Sanger High School, Sanger*

Apple Crumb Pie

5-7 tart apples
1 9" unbaked pastry shell
½ cup sugar
1 teaspoon cinnamon

½ cup sugar
¾ cup flour
⅓ cup butter

Pare apples and cut into eighths; arrange in pie shell. Combine ½ cup sugar with cinnamon and sprinkle over apples. Combine ½ cup sugar with flour and cut in butter. Sprinkle over apples. Bake in 400°F oven for 40 minutes. Serves 8.

Ellen Derby   *Tierra Del Sol School, San Diego*

Brownie Bottom Chantilly Pie

½ cup butter
2 squares of semi-sweet chocolate
1 cup sugar
2 eggs, beaten

1 teaspoon vanilla
¾ cup flour
½ cup chopped walnuts

Chantilly Cream:
1 cup whipping cream
¼ cup powdered sugar
½ teaspoon vanilla

1 cup sour cream
grated chocolate Hershey bar or
    chocolate cookies, crumbled

Preheat oven to 325°F. For brownie layer, melt butter and chocolate in a medium-sized saucepan over low heat, stirring occasionally. Stir in sugar, cool to room temperature. Stir in eggs and vanilla. Stir in flour and nuts until well-blended. Pour batter into a buttered 10" pie pan. Bake 30-35 minutes, or until wooden pick inserted in center comes out clean. Cool completely on wire rack.

One to two hours before serving, make chantilly cream. Whip cream in a small chilled bowl with chilled beaters until soft peaks form. Add powdered sugar and vanilla. Continue beating until stiff. Gently fold in sour cream. Spread over brownie layer, mounding slightly in the center. Decorate with grated Hershey bar or crumbled chocolate cookies. Serves 8.

Merideth Marcus   *San Pasqual High School, Escondido*

Two-Crust Banana Pie

4 cups bananas
½ cup pineapple juice
1 teaspoon cinnamon

½ cup sugar
1 tablespoon butter
double pie crust

Soak bananas in pineapple juice for 20 minutes. Drain and place in uncooked pie shell. On top of the bananas place 2 tablespoons pineapple juice, 1 teaspoon cinnamon and ½ cup sugar. Dot with butter. Place crust on top and cook at 400°F for 30-40 minutes. Serves 8.

"Here's a yummy pie that your guests have probably never tried before. Try it a la mode."
Pat Millard   *Valencia High School, Placentia*

94

Pineapple-Sour Cream Pie

1 9" baked pie shell	1 cup sour cream
1 cup sugar	2 egg yolks, slightly beaten
¼ cup flour	2 egg whites
½ teaspoon salt	½ teaspoon vanilla extract
1 20-oz. can crushed pineapple, drained	¼ teaspoon cream of tartar

Combine ¾ cup sugar, flour, and salt in saucepan. Stir in the drained pineapple and sour cream. Bring to a boil, stirring constantly. Cook for 2 minutes longer. Stir a small amount of hot mixture into egg yolks; stir egg yolks into hot mixture. Cook for 2 minutes, stirring constantly. Cool to room temperature. Spoon into pie shell. Beat egg whites, vanilla and cream of tartar in bowl until soft peaks form. Add ¼ cup sugar gradually, beating until stiff. Spread over pie, covering completely. Bake at 350°F for 12-15 minutes. Serves 6.

"A rich delightful combination of pineapple and sour cream with a meringue."

Phyllis J. Miller   **Buena High School, Ventura**

Raspberry Cream Pie

1 unbaked pie shell	1 cup sour cream
12 oz. cream cheese	10 oz. frozen raspberries, thawed
½ cup sugar	2 ½ to 3 teaspoons cornstarch
2 eggs	½ cup cream, whipped & sweetened to taste

Combine cream cheese, sugar and eggs and pour into pie shell. Bake at 375°F for 30 minutes. Cool. Spread top of pie with sour cream. Mix thawed raspberries and cornstarch; cook until thick. Cool. Fold whipped cream into raspberry mixture. Spoon mixture over pie and chill.

"Not too sweet! Great dessert!"

Gloria Reece   **Porterville High School, Porterville**

Luscious Lemon Pie

1 baked pie shell (9")	3 egg yolks, unbeaten
1 cup sugar	1 cup milk
3 tablespoons cornstarch	1 cup Dairy sour cream
¼ cup butter	whipped cream
1 tablespoon grated lemon rind	2 tablespoons walnuts, chopped
¼ cup lemon juice	

Combine sugar and cornstarch in saucepan. Add butter, lemon rind and juice, egg yolks, stir in milk. Cook over medium heat, stirring constantly, until thick. Cool. Fold in sour cream. Spoon into baked shell. Chill at least 2 hours. Serve with whipped cream and walnuts. Serves 6-8.

Linda Tsutsui   **Hanford High School, Hanford**

Pumpkin Pie Dessert

1 pkg. yellow cake mix
  (reserve 1 cup to be used in the topping)
½ cup melted butter
1 egg
1 can Libby's pumpkin (1 lb. 14 oz.)
½ cup sugar mixed with ¼ teaspoon salt
1 teaspoon cinnamon
¼ teaspoon cloves or allspice
¼ teaspoon ginger
2 eggs
1 small can evaporated milk

Topping:
1 cup cake mix
¼ cup sugar
½ teaspoon cinnamon
¼ cup melted butter
1 cup chopped nuts

Preheat oven to 350°.

Combine cake mix, ½ cup melted butter and 1 egg. Press into a 9 x 13" cake pan. Combine pumpkin, sugar, salt, cinnamon, cloves or allspice, ginger, 2 eggs, and 1 small can evaporated milk which have been beaten together until smooth. Pour over bottom layer. Bake 20 minutes. Remove from oven. Mix until crumbly, 1 cup cake mix, ¼ cup sugar, cinnamon, melted butter and 1 cup chopped nuts. Sprinkle on top of pie and return to oven and bake 30 minutes or until a toothpick comes out clean. Serve with whipped topping. Serves 24.

"This originated from one of the students in my foods class. Even people who 'don't like pumpkin pie' love this dessert!"
Mary Kantola   *Matthew Gage Middle School, Riverside*

Coconut Pie

¾ cup sugar
¼ cup cornstarch
⅛ teaspoon salt
2 cups milk
3 egg yolks
1 teaspoon vanilla

2 tablespoons butter
1 cup shredded coconut
1 baked pastry shell
3 egg whites
2 tablespoons confectioner's sugar
1 teaspoon vanilla

Mix sugar, cornstarch and salt well. Add milk and cook in double boiler or heavy aluminum pan. When the mixture first begins to thicken, add the egg yolks and continue to cook and stir until it reaches the desired thickness. Remove from stove, add vanilla, butter and most of the coconut. Pour into baked pie shell. While the filling is hot, cover with a meringue made from the three stiffly beaten egg whites, confectioner's sugar and vanilla have been added. Seal carefully, sprinkle the top with the reserved coconut and bake at 350° for 10-15 minutes. Serves 6-8.

"I use the standard single crust pastry recipe of 1 ¼ cups sifted all-purpose flour, ½ teaspoon salt, ½ cup Crisco or vegetable shortening, and 2-3 tablespoons cold water."
Yvonne Williams   *Warner School, Westminster*

Naked Apple Pie

1 egg
1/3 cup brown sugar
1/2 cup granulated sugar
1 teaspoon vanilla
1/8 teaspoon salt
1 teaspoon baking powder

1/2 cup flour
2-3 medium apples, pared and sliced
1/2 cup walnuts
1/8 teaspoon cinnamon
1/8 teaspoon nutmeg

Mix all ingredients well and spread in a greased 9" pie pan. Bake for 30 minutes at 350°F. Serve with whipped cream, if desired. Especially good hot. Serves 6.

Madelyn V. Fielding   **Jordan High School, Long Beach**

Lemon Cloud

1 can Eagle brand condensed milk
1 8-oz. carton Cool Whip
1 6-oz. can frozen lemonade

1 16-oz. can crushed pineapple, well-drained
2 graham cracker pie crust

Mix all ingredients together. Pour into 2 pie crust. Serves 12.

"Quick and Easy!"
Doris Waller   **Chino High School, Chino**

Mom's Cream-O-Peach Pie

3 fresh peaches, peeled and cut in half
  (canned could be used)
1 unbaked pie crust

3 tablespoons flour
3/4 cup sugar
1 cup heavy cream

Pre-heat oven at 425°F.

Place peach halves in crust cut side down. Mix flour and sugar together. Sprinkle over peaches. Pour cream over and around peaches. Bake at 425°F for 10 minutes. Reduce heat to 350°F. Bake 45 minutes. Serves 6.

"Great warm or cold — (if it lasts that long)! A favorite for over 30 years!! And so easy!!
Angie Garrett   **Tenaya Middle School, Fresno**

Fresh Strawberry Pie

4 12-oz. boxes whole strawberries, hulled
1 cup water
1 cup sugar
4 tablespoons cornstarch

1/8 teaspoon salt
1 tablespoon lemon juice
1 9" plain pastry pie shell, baked

Crush one box of berries in saucepan. Add water and bring to a boil. Simmer two minutes; strain. Add water to make 1 1/2 cups. Combine sugar, cornstarch and salt with juice. Cook three minutes, stirring constantly until thick and clear. Cool slightly. Arrange remaining berries in baked pastry shell. Spread glaze over berries, covering completely. Chill. When serving, garnish pieces with whipped cream. Serves 6.

Barbara Pruyne   **El Cajon Valley High School, El Cajon**

Raspberry Mousse Meringue Pie

4 egg whites
¼ teaspoon salt
1 ½ cups sugar
⅓ cup sliced almonds

2 10-oz. pkgs frozen raspberries, thawed
2 envelopes unflavored gelatin
1 cup Amaretto di Sarrono
2 cups (1 pint) heavy cream, whipped

Place egg whites in a large bowl, let warm to room temperature. Beat egg whites and salt until stiff. Beat in sugar, 1 tablespoon at a time, until meringue is stiff and glossy. Spread ⅔ of the mixture evenly over the bottom and sides of an 11" pie pan, place remaining meringue in a pastry bag fitted with a star tip. Press rosettes of meringue on the outer edge of pie pan, sprinkle shell with sliced almonds. Bake in pre-heated slow oven at 275°F for 40-45 minutes, or until lightly browned and hard to the touch. Turn off the oven and let shell cool in oven.

Whirl raspberries in a blender. Press puree through a sieve and remove seeds, then place puree in a saucepan. Stir in gelatin; stir over low heat until gelatin is dissolved. Stir in Amaretto di Sarrono and chill until syrupy. Fold in whipped cream; chill until mixture mounds. Mount filling into pie shell and garnish with whole raspberries. Chill until ready to serve and filling is firm. Serves 8.

Mary Conant   *Grandview School, Valinda*

Chocolate Pecan Pie

1 cup sifted flour
½ teaspoons salt
⅛ teaspoon baking powder

6 tablespoons shortening
2-3 tablespoons water

Filling:
⅓ cup butter, melted
3 eggs
1 cup packed light brown sugar
¼ teaspoon salt

½ teaspoon vanilla extract
3 oz. melted semi-sweet chocolate
1 cup light corn syrup
1 ⅓ cups pecan halves and pieces

Combine flour, salt and baking powder in a bowl. With a pastry blender, cut in shortening until uniform but fairly coarse. Sprinkle with water, a tablespoon at a time; toss with fork. Work dough into a firm ball. On a lightly floured surface, roll out crust 1 ½" larger than pie plate. Gently ease dough onto plate. Trim edge even with plate and flute.

In medium bowl, combine butter, eggs, brown sugar, salt and vanilla. Beat with a wire whip or rotary beater until smooth. Add melted chocolate. Stir in corn syrup until blended, making as little foam as possible. Fold in pecans. Pour into unbaked pie shell. Use blade of knife to arrange pecans rounded side up. Bake 49 to 50 minutes in 350°F oven or until filling is set. Cool slightly. Serve warm or cool. Serves 8.

Variations: Pecan pie — omit melted chocolate. Nut pie — substitute any unsalted nuts for the pecans.

Mary Lash   *Paramount High School, Paramount*

Florida Pie

6 egg whites
1 cup sugar
1 teaspoon vanilla
40 Ritz crushed crackers
½ cup chopped nuts
1 cup sugar
½ cup cocoa

½ cup butter
2 cups powdered sugar
2 eggs
1 teaspoon vanilla
1 pint whipping cream
6 tablespoons sugar
sweet chocolate curls

Beat egg whites until stiff. Gradually add 1 cup sugar and beat again. Add vanilla. Set aside. Mix crushed crackers, nuts and 1 cup sugar and fold into egg white mixture. Spread into a 9 x 13″ buttered pan. Bake at 350°F for 30 minutes. Cool 1 hour.

Combine in mixer bowl, cocoa, butter, powdered sugar and eggs. Beat until fluffy. Add 1 teaspoon vanilla. Spread over cooled meringue. Whip cream with sugar until stiff. Spread over chocolate mixture and garnish with chocolate curls. Refrigerate until ready to serve. Serves 12.

Donna Neel   *Orangeview Junior High School, Anaheim*

Cool Chocolate Cream Pie

⅓ cup cornstarch
1 ¾ cups milk
¼ teaspoon salt
1 cup chocolate syrup

2 egg yolks, slightly beaten
1 teaspoon vanilla
8-inch crumb crust or baked pastry shell

Combine cornstarch, milk, salt, syrup and egg yolks in medium micro-proof bowl. Microwave on medium-high (⅔ power) for 6 to 8 minutes, stirring every 2 minutes with wire whisk, until mixture boils and is thickened. Stir in vanilla. Pour into crust; press plastic wrap down on pie surface. Chill several hours or overnight until firm. Garnish with whipped topping, if desired.

Conventional Method: Combine cornstarch, milk, salt, chocolate syrup and egg yolks in medium saucepan. Cook, stirring constantly, until mixture boils and is thickened. Remove from heat and complete as in preceding recipe.

Hershey Foods Corporation   *Hershey, Pennsylvania*

Mud Pie

Oreo cookies (1 pkg.)
1 pint coffee ice cream
1 jar caramel topping

Cool Whip
sliced almonds

Crush Oreo cookies (filling and all) and press into a 9″ pie tin. Bake at 350°F for 20 minutes. Cool. Soften coffee ice cream and fill pie tin. Smooth it in. Pour caramel on top. Frost with cool whip and sprinkle almonds on top. Freeze until firm. Let sit a few minutes at room temperature before serving. Serves 6-8.

Cheré Brown   *Maricopa Unified High School, Maricopa*

Strawberry Pizza

2 baskets strawberries
½ cup sugar
½ cup water
1 cup flour
½ cup softened butter
3 tablespoons powdered sugar
8 ounces cream cheese
½ cup sugar

2 eggs
1 tablespoon lemon juice
1 tablespoon cornstarch
¼ cup sugar
1 cup juice from drained strawberries
1 tablespoon lemon juice
red food coloring

Slice strawberries; cover with ½ cup sugar and ¼ cup water. Let stand 2-3 hours. Drain well, reserving juice. Mix together flour, butter and powdered sugar with electric mixer until well-blended. Press into greased pizza pan with flat of hand; flute edges, and bake at 350°F for 10-12 minutes. Crust will not be brown, but will be firm. While crust is baking, cream cheese and ½ cup sugar together until fluffy; add eggs one at a time. Beat in lemon juice. Pour cream mixture into hot crust, spreading evenly. Bake at 350°F for 10-12 minutes until firm. Cool. Mix cornstarch and ¼ cup sugar together. Pour 1 cup strawberry juice over sugar. Stir until melted; add lemon juice. Bring to a boil and cook until thickened and clear. Add enough food coloring as needed to achieve desired color. Cool. Pour over strawberries to glaze. Place strawberries evenly over pizza. Chill well. Decorate with whipped cream. Serves 6-8.

"This is a luscious dessert that will get raves everywhere you serve it!"
Carole Delap   **Golden West High School, Visalia**

Butter Crunch Ice Cream Pie

½ cup butter
¼ cup brown sugar
1 cup flour
½ cup chopped nuts

1 pint vanilla ice cream
1 cup milk
1 package banana instant pudding

Heat oven to 400°F. Mix butter, brown sugar, flour and nuts together with hands. Spread in an oblong pan (13 x 9 ½ x 2"). Bake 15 minutes. Take from oven, stir with spoon. Save ¾ cup for topping. Immediately press rest of mixture against bottom and sides of a 9" pie pan. Cool. Beat until just mixed: ice cream, milk and instant pudding (approximately one minute). Pour at once into the 9" pie shell. Sprinkle reserved crumbs over top. Chill 1 hour. Serves 8.

"Suggested combinations: Chocolate instant pudding with vanilla ice cream; lemon pudding with pineapple ice cream; vanilla pudding with pistachio ice cream; strawberry pudding with strawberry ice cream. Can be made ahead, frozen and cut when partially thawed."
Myra Cochran   **Yuba City High School, Yuba City**

Lemon Refrigerator Pie

1 graham cracker pie crust (9")
2 eggs
rind of 1 lemon

1 can condensed milk
½ cup lemon juice

Bake crust for 10-15 minutes at 350°F, set aside to cool. Separate the egg yolks from whites. Beat the egg yolks very well and beat the whites until stiff peaks are formed. In a large bowl, combine the lemon rind, egg yolks, condensed milk, and ½ cup lemon juice until well-blended. Fold in the egg whites into the egg yolk mixture. Pour mixture into cooled crust. Bake at 350°F for 15 minutes. Cool and refrigerate for 24 hours. Serves 8.

"For garnish, sprinkle ¼ cup crushed graham cracker crumbs on top of pie."
Claudia J. Armstead   **Jefferson Junior High School, Long Beach**

Margarita Pie

Crust:

5 tablespoons butter
½ cup pretzel crumbs

½ cup vanilla wafer crumbs
3 tablespoons sugar

Filling:

1 envelope unflavored gelatin
1 teaspoon grated lemon peel
7 tablespoons freshly
  squeezed lemon juice
5 egg yolks
½ cup sugar

¼ teaspoon salt
5 tablespoons tequila
2 tablespoons plus 2 teaspoons triple sec
5 egg whites
7 tablespoons sugar
1 lemon unpeeled, thinly cut in cartwheels

Melt butter in a 9″ pie plate. Add crumbs and sugar. Mix well. Press mixture into bottom and sides of pie plate.

Soften gelatin in mixture of lemon peel and juice. Cook slowly, about 3 minutes. Do not boil. Beat egg yolks in pyrex bowl until very thick; beat in ½ cup sugar and salt. Add gelatin mixture and cook until slightly thickened. Stir and add liquors. Chill over ice water or in refrigerator, stirring frequently until cooled (mixture should not be too thick). Beat egg whites to soft-peak stage. Gradually beat in 7 tablespoons sugar at high speed until all sugar is used. Whites should be glossy and moist and tips of peaks should fall slightly when beater is withdrawn. Carefully fold yolk mixture into whites. Spoon into pretzel crust. Arrange lemon cartwheels around edge of pie. Chill until firm. Serve the *same day* it is made or it will become rubbery. Make 6-8 servings.

"Excellent dessert for after a Mexican-style meal or buffet dinner."
Carleen Street   **Wasco Union High School, Wasco**

Fudge Pie

¼ cup cocoa
¼ cup flour
1 cup sugar
2 eggs

1 teaspoon vanilla
½ cup butter (melted)
1 unbaked pastry shell

Mix all ingredients together. Pour into unbaked pastry shell. Bake in 375°F oven for 25 to 30 minutes. Serves 6.

"Excellent served warm with scoop of French Vanilla ice cream."
Nancy Voyles   **Canyon High School, Anaheim**

Surprise Creme Pie

Crust:
5 tablespoons butter
1 ¼ cups finely crushed graham crackers
¼ cup sugar
2 oz. of milk chocolate candy bars

Filling:
1 5-oz. pkg regular vanilla pudding mix
3 cups milk
2 egg yolks

Meringue
2 egg whites
½ teaspoon vanilla
½ teaspoon cream of tartar
¼ cup sugar

Do all cooking on 100% setting in the microwave oven.

Prepare crumb crust: In a 9″ pie plate micro-melt 5 tablespoons butter, about 45 seconds. Stir in 1 ¼ cups finely crushed graham crackers and ¼ cup sugar. Press over bottom and sides of pie plate. Micro-cook, uncovered, 2 minutes, turning dish after 1 minute.

Break up two 1 ounce milk chocolate candy bars and arrange over hot crust; spread until smooth. Set crust aside.

In a 4-cup glass measure combine a 5-oz. package of regular vanilla pudding mix and 3 cups of milk. Micro-cook, uncovered, 3 minutes. Stir. Micro-cook, uncovered until pudding thickens and bubbles, about 2 to 3 minutes more, stirring after each minute. Stir half of the hot pudding into 2 slightly beaten egg yolks. Return to hot mixture. Micro-cook 1 minute more. Pour into prepared crust.

In small bowl beat 2 egg whites with ½ teaspoon vanilla and ¼ teaspoon cream of tartar until soft peaks form. Gradually add ¼ cup sugar, beating till stiff peaks form. Spread atop pie, sealing to edges of crust.

Under infrared Browning Unit: *Do not preheat unit.* Brown pie about 3 to 4 minutes, turning pie for even browning as necessary. Cool. If you don't have a microwave browning element, this may be browned in a regular oven at 400°F for about 8-10 minutes. Serves 8.

Polly Frank   *Lakewood High School, Lakewood*

Walnut Pie

3 egg whites
1 cup granulated sugar
1 teaspoon vanilla
14 soda crackers, crushed

½ teaspoon baking powder
1 cup walnuts
whipped cream

Beat egg whites until stiff; add sugar, vanilla, crushed soda crackers and baking powder. Fold in nuts. Bake in lightly greased 9″ pie pan at 325°F for 45 minutes. Serve with whipped cream. Serves 6-8.

Helen M. Stump   *Vina Danks Middle School, Ontario*

Easy Grasshopper Pie

2 cups chocolate wafer crumbs
(approx. 8 ½-oz. pkg.)
⅓ cup butter or margarine, melted
⅔ cup milk
40 large marshmallows (10-oz. pkg)

⅓ cup green creme de menthe
¼ cup white creme de cacao
2 cups whipping cream
5 drops green food coloring

Combine crumbs and melted butter. Reserve about 2 tablespoons for topping. Press remainder into buttered 10" pie plate. Bake at 350°F for 8 to 10 minutes. Cool. In a 3-quart pan, over low heat, stir milk and marshmallows until they melt. Cool. Chill for a few minutes until it thickens. Stir until smooth. Stir in liqueurs. Beat cream until stiff. Fold marshmallow mixture into whipped cream. Fold in food color. Pour into crust. Sprinkle with reserved crumbs. Freeze or chill about 3 hours until set. Serves 8.

"This can be served chilled or frozen."
Bonnie Shrock   **Kearny High School, San Diego**

Chocolate Cheese Pie

1 ½ cups graham cracker crumbs
½ cup melted butter
1 6-oz. pkg chocolate chips
2 3-oz. pkgs cream cheese
½ cup sugar

1 teaspoon vanilla
¼ teaspoon salt
2 eggs (separated)
1 cup whipping cream
¼ cup sugar

Make crumb crust of graham crackers and butter. Pat in a 9" pan. Chill. Melt chocolate chips over hot water, cool slightly. Stir cream cheese to soften; blend in sugar, vanilla and salt. Add egg yolks one at a time; beat well. Stir in chocolate and chill until thick. Beat smooth. Whip cream and fold into the chocolate mixture. Beat egg whites, add ¼ cup sugar and fold into chocolate. Pour into crust and freeze. Remove from freezer 5-10 minutes before serving. Serves 6.

"This is best if served partially frozen."
Denise Hammond   **Yuba City High School, Yuba City**

Pear Crumble Pie

6 medium pears, pared
3 tablespoons lemon juice
½ cup sugar
2 tablespoons all-purpose flour
1 teaspoon grated lemon peel
1 unbaked 9" pastry shell
3 slices sharp American cheese

Crumble Topping:
½ cup all-purpose flour
½ cup sugar
½ teaspoon ginger
½ teaspoon cinnamon
¼ teaspoon mace
4 tablespoons butter

Slice 5 pears; cut remaining pear into sixths. Sprinkle pears with lemon juice. Mix sugar, flour and lemon peel; stir into sliced pears. Spoon into pastry shell. Arrange pear wedges atop sliced pears. Sprinkle with crumble topping. Place slices of American cheese on top. Bake at 400°F oven for 45 minutes.

Bonnie Smith   **Tustin High School, Tustin**

Black Bottom Pie

⅓ cup butter
20 graham crackers
¼ cup sugar

Filling:
1 tablespoon unflavored gelatin
¼ cup cold water
2 cups milk
4 eggs
2 cups sugar
2 tablespoons cornstarch
1 cup chocolate chips
¾ teaspoon vanilla
¾ teaspoon rum or vanilla flavoring

Crush graham crackers; mix with sugar and butter. Pat into pie pan. Bake at 375°F for 8 minutes.

Sprinkle gelatin over cold water. Heat milk until film forms across the top. Separate eggs. Beat yolks until bubbly. Slowly add milk into eggs. Mix ¼ cup sugar and cornstarch together; stir into milk. Place over boiling water, and cook, stirring constantly until mixture thickly coats a silver spoon.

Measure ⅔ cup cooked custard into a bowl. Add chocolate chips, vanilla and beat until well-blended. Pour into cooled pie shell; chill. Stir softened gelatin into remaining custard. Continue stirring until gelatin is dissolved. Chill until mixture is slightly thicker than consistency of unbeaten egg whites.

Beat egg whites until stiff enough to hold soft peaks. Add remaining sugar gradually, beating until egg whites form stiff peaks. Gently stir in gelatin, custard mixture, rum or vanilla flavoring. Spoon over chocolate layer. Chill until firm. Shave chocolate curls thinly and serve garnished with whipped cream and chocolate curls. Serves 6-8.

Roberta Priestley   *Alhambra High School, Alhambra*

Chocolate Amaretto Pie

8-oz. almond Hershey bar
2 oz. creme de cacao
1 ½ oz. Amaretto

8 oz. Cool Whip
1 chocolate or graham crust or
    OREO chocolate cookie crust*

Melt 8 oz. almond Hershey bar in double boiler. Add creme de cacao and Amaretto. Cool. Fold in 8 oz. Cool Whip. Pour into chocolate or graham crust. Serve chilled. Serves 4-6.

"A favorite of chocolate and almond fans."

*Oreo Chocolate Cookie Crust: In a blender crumb 20 Oreo chocolate cookies. (The icing serves as the sugar). Melt ¼ cup butter or margarine. Mix. Press into pie tin or 8" square.

Betty Patterson   *Lakewood High School, Lakewood*

Black Russian Pie

24 large marshmallows
½ cup cold milk
⅛ teaspoon salt

¼ cup kahlua
1 cup whipping cream
1 chocolate cookie crust (9″)

Melt marshmallows in double boiler with milk and salt (or melt in microwave in glass bowl on high, stirring once until melted). Let cool. Stir in ¼ cup of kahlua. Whip the cream and fold into the marshmallow mixture. Refrigerate for 30 minutes. Put in pie shell and freeze. Top with chocolate shot or chocolate curls. Serves 6-8.

"A good make-ahead company recipe".
Ruth Long
Clovis West High School, Fresno

Chocolate Charlotte Pie

1 12-oz. bag chocolate chips
1 cup whipping cream
3 tablespoons sugar
3 eggs
1 teaspoon vanilla

pinch of salt
1 baked 8″ pie shell
whipped cream and slivered almonds
  for topping

Melt chocolate chips in double boiler over hot, not boiling water or in microwave according to directions. Meanwhile, beat cream until stiff adding sugar one tablespoon at a time, beating after each addition. Pour melted chocolate into large bowl. Add eggs one at a time, beating on medium high speed. Beat in vanilla and salt. Fold in whipped cream. Pour into baked pie shell. Top with additional whipped cream and toasted slivered almonds. Serves 12.

"For chocoholics use a chocolate crust. This pie is sinfully rich and yummy!"
Jane McPhee
Fountain Valley High School, Fountain Valley

Peanut Butter Pie

¾ cup confectioner's sugar
½ cup creamy peanut butter
1 baked 9″ pastry shell
½ cup sugar
¼ cup cornstarch

½ teaspoon salt
2 ½ cups milk
3 eggs (separated)
1 teaspoon vanilla
6 tablespoons sugar

Mix confectioner's sugar and peanut butter until crumbs form. Cover bottom of pastry shell with crumbs, reserving about 3 tablespoons for the top. Mix together sugar, cornstarch and salt in saucepan. Stir in milk and egg yolks. Cook over medium heat, stirring constantly, until mixture comes to a boil and boils one minute. Remove from heat. Stir in vanilla. Cool. Spoon into prepared pastry shell. Beat egg whites until foamy. Add sugar, 1 tablespoon at a time, beating well after each addition. Continue beating until stiff peaks form when beater is raised. Spread on top of filling. Bake 7 minutes or until brown in a 400°F oven.

Gwen Hansen
Bloomington High School, Bloomington

Fudge Chiffon Pie

9-inch baked pastry shell or crumb crust
1 envelope unflavored gelatin
¼ cup cold water
¾ cup boiling water
⅛ teaspoon salt

3-oz. pkg. cream cheese
1 ½ cups (1-lb. can) chocolate
½ cup fudge topping
3 egg whites
2 tablespoons sugar

Prepare pastry shell or crumb crust; set aside.

Sprinkle gelatine onto cold water in a small bowl; allow to soften. Add boiling water and salt; stir until dissolved.

In small mixer bowl beat cream cheese until smooth; add fudge topping beating until well-blended. Gradually add gelatine mixture; chill until set.

In another small mixer bowl beat egg whites with sugar until stiff peaks form. Beat chocolate mixture until smooth; carefully fold in egg whites. Pour into pastry shell, crumb crust or chocolate cups. Chill thoroughly. Garnish with sweetened whipped cream or dessert topping and fresh fruit, if desired.

Hershey Foods Corporation   *Hershey, Pennsylvania*

Bishop's Chocolate Pie

1 stick margarine
1 cup flour
¼ cup chopped pecans
¼ cup brown sugar
1 pkg. instant vanilla pudding

1 pkg. instant chocolate pudding
2 cups milk
2 cups vanilla ice cream, softened a little
1 large Cool Whip
large Hershey bar

Mix margarine, flour, pecans, and brown sugar in a bowl. Pat out on jelly roll pan for crust. Bake at 350°F for 15 minutes. Let cool. Mix puddings, milk and ice cream; pour over crust. Refrigerate. Top with 1 large carton of Cool Whip and shaved Hershey Bar. Note: Be sure to use jelly roll pan not pie plate. Serves 6.

"This recipe is from Bishop's Cafeteria in the Midwest."
Nancy Bryant   *Buena Park High School, Buena Park*

Almond Tarts

1 ⅓ cup butter or margarine
⅔ cup sugar
2 egg yolks

1 cup ground almonds
3 cups flour
½ teaspoon almond extract

Cream butter and sugar until light. Mix in egg yolk and ground almonds. (Almonds must be fine). Sift flour and mix into butter mixture. Add flavoring. Roll into rolls 1 inch in diameter; roll in waxed paper and chill. Cut off ¾" thick pieces and press into tart pans that have 2 strips of paper towels criss-crossed in the bottom of the pan. Dough should be about ¼" thick. Bake in 325° oven for 12 minutes. Remove by lifting on papers. When cool fill with pudding or fruit.

Emily Lewis   *Cerritos High School, Cerritos*

Recipe for "Marble Chiffon Cake" on page 16 ➡
Recipe for "Fudge Chiffon Pie" on page 106 ➡

Maple Nut Pizza

Pastry for a two-crusted pie
½ cup margarine
1 cup sugar
2 eggs

2 cups chopped nuts
   (walnuts or pecans)
1 teaspoon vanilla
½ cup maple-flavored syrup

Roll pastry to fit bottom of a 14″ pizza pan. Fit dough loosely and have a half inch side edge.

Cream together margarine, sugar, eggs, then all walnuts and vanilla. Blend well and pour over pie crust. Drizzle syrup over batter. Bake at 375°F for 25 minutes. Cool. Cut into wedges and serve. Serves 15-20.

"Can be frozen."
Leona L. Rice   *Ahwahnee Middle School, Fresno*

Our Mother's Old Fashioned Butterscotch Pie

1 tablespoon butter
1 tablespoon flour
2 egg yolks
1 ¾ cups milk
1 cup brown sugar, packed

1 9″ baked pie shell
2 egg whites
¼ teaspoon cream of tartar
¼ cup sugar
¼ teaspoon vanilla

Brown butter well . . . this is important. Add flour and continue to cook 1 to 2 minutes longer. Beat egg yolks well in saucepan; add milk, brown sugar, and flour mixture. Cook over medium heat until mixture is smooth and stiff. Cool and pour into pie shell. Beat egg whites until foamy with cream of tartar. Add sugar gradually, beating until stiff; add vanilla. Bake at 400°F for 8 to 10 minutes until meringue is brown.
Sharon Schooping   *El Dorado High School, Placentia*

Paradise Pumpkin Pie

8-oz. pkg cream cheese
¼ cup sugar
½ teaspoon vanilla
1 egg
9″ unbaked pie crust
1 ¼ cups canned pumpkin
½ cup sugar
1 teaspoon cinnamon

¼ teaspoon ginger
¼ teaspoon nutmeg
dash of salt
1 cup evaporated milk
2 eggs
nuts (optional)
maple syrup and nuts for topping

Heat oven to 350°F. Combine cream cheese, sugar and vanilla. Mix well. Add egg; blend and spread over bottom of pastry shell. Combine remaining ingredients; mix well. Carefully pour over cream cheese mixture. Bake one hour and 5 minutes, or until done. Cool; brush with maple syrup, garnish with nuts. Serves 8.

Peggy Adams   *Paramount High School, Paramount*

← Recipe for "Cool Chocolate Souffle" on page 114
← Recipe for "Cool Chocolate Cream Pie" on page 99

Eggnog Chiffon Pie

1 envelope (1 tablespoon)
   unflavored gelatin
¼ cup milk
1 ½ cups dairy eggnog
3 eggs
½ cup sugar

½ teaspoon vanilla
1 9" pie shell, baked and cooled
1 cup whipped cream
2 tablespoons sugar
1 square semi-sweet chocolate
   (for making chocolate curls)

Soften gelatin in milk for 5 minutes. Heat eggnog in saucepan over low heat. Separate eggs and beat yolks well, adding ¼ cup sugar as you beat. Pour mixture into heated eggnog and cook over hot, not boiling water. Stir until mixture coats a spoon. Remove from heat and add softened gelatin. Stir until completely dissolved and then cool. Beat egg whites until smooth, but not dry. Slowly add the remaining ¼ cup sugar, beating until stiff. Gently fold into cooled custard mixture along with vanilla. Chill in refrigerator until this begins to congeal. Pour into baked pie shell and chill until set. Garnish with whipped cream sweetened with 2 tablespoons sugar and chocolate curls. Pull peeler across chocolate square to make curls. Makes 1 9" pie.

"Curls will be easier to make if chocolate is slightly warmed up by holding in palm of hand tightly for a few minutes."
Charla Moore
                                          McLane High School, Fresno

Pecan Cream Cheese Pie

1 unbaked pie shell
16 oz. cream cheese
   (room temperature)
¼ cup sugar
1 egg
2 teaspoons vanilla

3 eggs
¾ cup light corn syrup
2 tablespoons sugar
1 teaspoon vanilla
3 oz. pecans, lightly toasted and
   finely chopped

Line pie crust with waxed paper; fill with dried beans and bake for 10 minutes in 350°F oven. Combine cream cheese, ¼ cup sugar, 1 egg and 2 teaspoons vanilla in mixing bowl; beat until smooth.

In another bowl, beat eggs, corn syrup, sugar and vanilla until well mixed. Pour cream cheese mixture into prebaked pie crust, spreading evenly. Sprinkle with pecans. Stir corn syrup mixture again and carefully pour over pecans (this prevents pecans from shifting). Bake until set about 40 minutes. Serve chilled. Serves 8.

Clara Bartlett
                       John W. North High School, Riverside

Pecan Pie

1 unbaked pie shell
⅓ cup butter (no substitution)
¾ cup brown sugar (firmly packed)
3 eggs

1 cup waffle syrup
1 cup chopped pecans
1 teaspoon vanilla
¼ teaspoon salt

Prepare an 8″ unbaked pie shell. Cream the butter and sugar. Beat in the eggs one at a time. Stir in the waffle syrup, pecans, vanilla and salt. Fill the shell. Decorate the top with some unbroken pecan halves. Bake in a moderate oven (375°F) for about ½ hour until the filling sets and the crust is golden brown. Serves 6.

"The flavor of the waffle syrup makes a big difference in this pie. In California, I use Log Cabin's 'Country Kitchen' waffle syrup. I use the Crisco single crust pastry recipe."
Yvonne Williams   **Warner School, Westminster**

Pie Shell Tarts

1 cup sifted flour   ⅓ cup shortening
¼ teaspoon salt   3 tablespoons cold water

Stir flour and salt together. Cut in shortening. Stir in water one tablespoon at a time, using a fork. Place dough in waxed paper, shape into a ball, then divide into 6 equal parts. Roll each part into a 5″ circle on a floured surface. Poke with a fork and shape dough on an upside down muffin pan. Pinch sides to shape over the muffin cups. Bake at 425°F for 10-12 minutes or until light brown. Remove and let cool. Fill with your favorite filling. Examples: fresh fruit, pie filling or pudding garnished with whipped cream; creamed beef or chicken; creamed vegetables; scrambled eggs with cheese. Serves 6.
JoAnne Bugh   **Rialto Junior High School, Rialto**

Pumpkin Chiffon Pie

1 envelope unflavored gelatin   ¾ cup milk
½ cup sugar   2 slightly beaten egg yolks
½ teaspoon salt   1 cup canned pumpkin
½ teaspoon ground cinnamon   2 egg whites
½ teaspoon ground allspice   ¼ cup sugar
¼ teaspoon ground ginger   ½ cup whipping cream, whipped
¼ teaspoon ground nutmeg   1 9″ graham-cracker pie crust**

Combine first 7 ingredients in saucepan. Stir in milk, egg yolks, and pumpkin. Cool and stir over medium heat until mixture boils and gelatin dissolves. Remove from heat and chill until partially set.

Beat egg whites till soft peaks form. Gradually add sugar and beat to stiff peaks. Fold into pumpkin mixture with whipped cream. Pile into crust. Chill until firm.

Graham cracker crust: 1 package graham crackers, ¼ cup butter and ¼ cup sugar. Finely roll graham crackers. Pour crumbs in a bowl. Add sugar and softened butter. Blend well with fork, fingers or pastry blender. Place in a 9″ pie pan and press firmly on bottom and sides. Bake in a moderate oven (375°F) for 8 minutes. Remove to wire rack to cool. Fill with filling above and chill.
Donna Swennes   **El Capitan High School, Lakeside**

Sky High Lemon Chiffon Pie

1 9" baked pastry shell
1 envelope Knox unflavored gelatin
¾ cup sugar
5 eggs, separated

½ cup water
½ cup lemon juice
1 teaspoon grated lemon peel

In medium saucepan, mix unflavored gelatin with ½ cup sugar. Blend in egg yolks beaten with water and lemon juice. Let stand 1 minute. Stir over low heat until gelatin is completely dissolved, about 5 minutes. Add lemon peel. Pour into large bowl and chill, stirring occasionally, until mixture mounds slightly when dropped from spoon. In medium bowl, beat egg whites until soft peaks form. Add remaining sugar and beat until stiff. Fold into gelatin mixture. Turn into prepared crust. Chill until firm. Garnish, if desired, with whipped cream and maraschino cherries.

"Cool, light, disappears in your mouth, and also from the pie pan!"
Lois Salisbury   **Mt. View High School, El Monte**

Puddings & Custards

Better Than Tom Selleck

1½ cubes margarine	1 cup powdered sugar
1 cup flour	1 cup Cool Whip
½ cup brown sugar	1 pkg instant vanilla pudding
¾ cup chopped pecans	1 pkg chocolate pudding
1 oz. cream cheese (softened)	3 cups milk

Mix together the first four ingredients and bake 325°F for 25 minutes. Stir several times. Reserve ½ cup of baked mixture for top and spread remainder on the bottom of a 9 x 13" baking dish. Cool. Mix cream cheese and powdered sugar and fold in Cool Whip. Spread over the bottom layer in baking dish. Spread with chocolate pudding made with 1 ½ cups milk. Spread with vanilla pudding made with 1 ½ cups milk. Sprinkle with reserved mix. Refrigerate until serving time. Serves 16-20.

Sharletta Kay Myers   *DeMille Jr. High School, Long Beach*

Cream Cheese Pudding

1 box instant pudding (any flavor)	1 8-oz. pkg. cream cheese
2 cups milk (I make 2 cups reconstituted non-fat dry milk)	

Put pudding mix and milk into blender. Cube cream cheese (1-inch cubes). Start blender, adding cream cheese cubes and add thru shoot while blender is operating (pudding will set up quickly in the blender, so work fast). Pour into serving dishes or pie shell. Refrigerate. Serves 4.

Sally Jean Artz   *Santa Fe Middle School, Monrovia*

Lemon Pineapple Créme

¾ cup sugar, divided	2 eggs, separated
3 tablespoons cornstarch	1 teaspoon grated lemon peel
1 8-oz. ˜an crushed pineapple, undrained	2 tablespoons lemon juice
⅔ cup water	1 3-oz. pkg. cream cheese, cubed

In a 4-cup glass measure bowl, mix ½ cup sugar, the cornstarch, pineapple and its juice, and water. Cook, uncovered on HI (max power) in microwave 4 to 5 minutes, or until mixture boils. Stir twice during cooking time. Beat egg yolks. Stir into pineapple mixture; add lemon peel, juice and egg yolks. Add cream cheese. Cook, uncovered on 80 (reheat) 1 minute. Beat with electric mixer to blend in cream cheese. Cool. Beat egg whites until frothy, gradually adding ¼ cup of sugar until soft peaks form. Fold into cooled pudding. Spoon into dessert dishes and refrigerate until served. Garnish with half a slice each of lemon and sprig of mint. Serves 5-6.

"A light, refreshing dessert."
Debbie Wilson   *Hueneme High School, Oxnard*

English Trifle

1 Jiffy cake mix, yellow	1 16-oz. pkg frozen strawberries
1 5¾-oz. pkg instant vanilla pudding mix	or fresh strawberries in season
	1 8-oz. container Cool Whip

Follow directions on package for cake mix and pudding mix. Alternate layers of the above ingredients in bite size pieces of cake, pudding, strawberries, and Cool Whip. The final layer should always be the Cool Whip. Garnish with a few strawberries. Serves 8-12.

"Use a clear salad bowl in order to see the layers of cake, pudding, strawberries and Cool Whip."
Kathie Baczynski   *Mt. Carmel High School, San Diego*

Persimmon Pudding

1 cup sugar
½ teaspoon salt
1 teaspoon baking powder
1 cup flour
1 teaspoon cinnamon
1 teaspoon soda

1 egg
¼ cup buttermilk or fruit juice
1 teaspoon vanilla
1 tablespoon oil
1 cup persimmon pulp
½ cup nuts

Sift together dry ingredients. Set aside. Beat egg, add milk or juice, vanilla, oil and persimmon pulp. Gradually combine dry ingredients with persimmon mixture. Sprinkle nuts on top of pudding and bake in a covered dish 350°F oven for 70 minutes. (Do not uncover until cooled).

"This can be made when persimmons are ripe and frozen for later use."
Janet Griffith   *Norco Senior High School, Norco*

Pots De Creme

¾ cup milk
1 cup semi-sweet chocolate pieces
1 egg
2 tablespoons sugar

1 teaspoon vanilla
⅛ teaspoon salt
whipped cream

Scald milk; do not boil. Combine all ingredients in blender and mix at medium speed until smooth. Pour into dessert dishes and chill several hours. Serve with dab of whipped cream on top.

"This is an extremely rich dessert, so serve in small dishes . . . looks elegant in crystal!"
Judi McEachen   *Lakewood High School, Lakewood*

Lemon Cake Pudding

¼ cup flour
1 cup sugar
¼ teaspoon salt
1 tablespoon grated lemon rind (1 lemon)

¼ cup lemon juice
2 egg yolks, well-beaten
1 cup milk
2 egg whites, stiffly beaten

Heat oven to 350°F (moderate). Blend flour, sugar and salt into mixing bowl. Stir in lemon rind and juice, egg yolks and milk. Fold in egg whites. Pour into 1-quart baking dish (6 ½"), or 6 custard cups. Set in pan of hot water (1 inch deep). Bake 50 minutes. Serves 6.

"Delicate cake and refreshing lemon sauce in one pudding!"
Dorothy Shirley   *Live Oak High School, Live Oak*

Persimmon Pudding

1 cup blended persimmon pulp
  (fully ripe, soft)
1 cup plus 2 tablespoons flour
1 cup granulated sugar
2 eggs
2 teaspoons soda
½ teaspoon salt
1 teaspoon cinnamon
¼ cup melted butter
1 teaspoon vanilla
½ cup chopped nuts (optional)
½ cup raisins, dates, or glace fruit (optional)

Lemon sauce:
1 cup granulated sugar
1 egg
½ cup melted butter
juice of 2 lemons
grated rind of 1 lemon
¼ teaspoon salt

Mix all ingredients together thoroughly. Pour into two well greased pudding molds or two 1-lb. coffee cans. Fill ⅔ full. Cover (waxed paper followed by foil does nicely for the cans). Set in boiling water; cover with a lid or foil. Bake in oven at 350°F for 1 ½ hours. Serve with Lemon Sauce: Mix all ingredients together. Cook in double boiler, stirring constantly, until thickened. Serves 12-14.

"The pudding may be baked in a well-greased loaf pan at 350°F for 1 hour, or until pick comes clean, but does not have the same texture as the other method. The oven-steaming does not steam the kitchen as badly as the top-stove type of steaming. The pudding freezes well also."
Betsy Cosart   **Monache High School, Porterville**

Cool Chocolate Soufflé

2 envelopes unflavored gelatin
½ cup water
6 egg yolks
¾ cup milk
3 tablespoons butter or margarine
1 ½ teaspoons vanilla

1 ½ cups (1-pound can) chocolate syrup
6 egg whites
¼ teaspoon cream of tartar
⅓ cup sugar
1 cup heavy cream (NOT whipped topping)

Measure length of aluminum foil to go around 1-quart souffle dish; fold in half lengthwise. Butter one side of collar; tape securely to outside of dish (buttered side in) allowing collar to extend 4 inches above rim of dish. Set aside. Soften gelatin in water in small bowl a few minutes. Slightly beat egg yolks in large microproof bowl; add milk, gelatin mixture, and butter or margarine. Microwave on medium-high (⅔ power) for 3 to 4 minutes, stirring once, just until mixture is very hot and coats a spoon. DO NOT BOIL. Blend in vanilla and chocolate syrup. Press plastic wrap onto surface. Cool; chill, stirring occasionally, until mixture mounds from spoon. Beat egg whites with cream of tartar in large mixer bowl until foamy; gradually add sugar, beating until stiff peaks form. Fold egg whites into chocolate mixture. Whip cream; fold in. Pour into prepared dish; cover and chill overnight. Just before serving, carefully remove foil collar. Garnish with dessert topping and fresh fruit, if desired. 12 to 14 servings.

Conventional Method: Soften gelatin in water in medium saucepan; add milk, egg yolks and butter. Cook stirring constantly, until mixture coats a spoon but does not boil. Remove from heat and complete as in preceding recipe.

Hershey Foods Corporation   **Hershey, Pennsylvania**

Lemon Layered Dessert

¼ lb. butter or margarine
1 cup flour
½ cup chopped walnuts
3 oz. lemon gelatin
8 oz. cream cheese

¾ cup granulated sugar
4 cups Cool Whip (or whipped cream)
3 cups milk
2 pkgs (3 ¾-oz.) lemon instant pudding

Mix together: butter, flour, nuts, and press into a 9 x 13″ pan. Bake at 350°F for 15-20 minutes or until lightly brown. Cool. Dissolve 3 oz. lemon gelatin in 1 cup hot water, cool. When gelatin is cool, add cream cheese, sugar and 2 cups of Cool Whip. Mix. Pour into cooled crust. Mix 3 cups milk with 2 packages lemon instant pudding. Mix until it is a pudding consistency. Spread on cream cheese layer. The last layer = 2 cups Cool Whip. Sprinkle with chopped nuts. Cover and refrigerate overnight. Serves 12-15.

Carolyn Crum   *Newhart School, Mission Viejo*

Dutch Babies

6 eggs
1 cup sifted flour
½ teaspoon salt
1 cup milk

4 tablespoons melted butter
lemon wedges
powdered sugar to taste

Using a french whisk, beat eggs until blended. Sift flour again with salt. Add flour and salt to eggs in 4 additions, beating after each. Add milk in 2 additions, beating after each. Lightly beat in cooled, melted butter. *Generously* grease baking pans. Fill each with 1/6 of the mixture. Bake in a hot oven (400°F) for 15 minutes; reduce heat to 350°F and bake 10 minutes more. Slip onto hot plates. Offer lemon wedges, powdered sugar. Serves 6.

"Six individual baking dishes are needed. I prefer pyrex soufflé dishes (1-pint capacity). Any 6″ baking pans or frying pans will do."
Martha Ford   *Roosevelt Junior High School, Glendale*

Lemon Lush (Short for Luscious)

1 cup sifted flour
1 cube butter or margarine
½ cup chopped nuts
1 cup sifted powdered sugar

1 large pkg cream cheese
1 cup Cool Whip
2 pkgs instant lemon pudding
3 cups milk

Mix together sifted flour, butter and chopped nuts. Press into an 8 x 8″ pan. Bake at 375°F until lightly browned. Cool completely. Mix together and spread over the cookie base: sifted powdered sugar, cream cheese and Cool Whip. Mix and pour over the cream cheese mixture, instant lemon pudding made with 3 cups of milk. Spread a thin layer of Cool Whip on top. Garnish with more chopped nuts if desired. Keep refrigerated. Serves 9.

"Always a delight after a meal."
Marcy Bergner   *Kearny High School, San Diego*

Chocolate Rum Mousse

1 cup flour
1 stick soft butter
½ cup nuts
8 oz. soft cream cheese
1 cup powdered sugar
9 oz. Cool Whip

2 regular pkgs. instant
   chocolate pudding
3 cups milk
3 teaspoons rum or rum flavoring
9-oz. carton of Cool Whip
¼ cup nut meats

Mix flour, butter and ½ cup nuts and pat into 9″ by 13″ pan. Bake 15 minutes at 350°. Cool. Mix cream cheese, powdered sugar and 9 ounces Cool Whip. Layer over 1st mixture. Mix 2 packages instant chocolate pudding, 3 cups milk and rum. Layer over the 2nd mixture. Top with another 9-oz. carton Cool Whip. Garnish with nuts. Chill. Serves 24.

"Can be frozen. Good for a party dessert."
Charlene M. Stott   **Horace Mann Jr. High School, San Diego**

Pudding Delight

1 ½ cups flour
¾ cup butter
1 cup walnuts
8 oz. cream cheese
1 cup Cool Whip

1 cup powdered sugar
1 small box instant vanilla pudding
1 small box instant chocolate pudding
3 cups milk
Hershey bar (optional)

Mix flour, butter and chopped walnuts. Press mixture into a 9 x 13″ cake pan. Bake 20 minutes at 350°. Cool. Beat with electric mixer: cream cheese, Cool Whip, and powdered sugar. Add a small amount of milk to help consistency. Spread mixture on crust. Beat both puddings and milk, 2 minutes. Spread on above mixture. Top with remaining Cool Whip. Optional — grate Hershey bar on top of dessert. Refrigerate at least 3 hours. Serves 15.

Amy Tyler Nosek   **Arroyo High School, El Monte**

Snow Balls

1 cup sugar
½ cup margarine
2 egg yolks
⅔ cup drained crushed pineapple

1 cup nuts
2 egg whites (beaten)
½ box vanilla wafers
1 carton of whipping cream

Cream sugar, margarine and eggs. Add drained pineapple and nuts. Fold in beaten egg whites. Place vanilla wafers with round side down in the dish (across the bottom of the entire dish). Spread half of the cream mixture over the vanilla wafers; place another layer of vanilla wafers on the cream mixture. Layer of cream and top with whipping cream. (Dish or pan size 13 x 9 x 2).

"This recipe should be prepared at least 24 hours before you intend to use it. Stays nice for at least 7 days in the refrigerator. Recipe at least 30 years old!"
Antoinette DeNeve   **Jones Junior High School, Baldwin Park**

Mother's Dilemma

Crust:
½ cup butter or margarine
1 ¼ cup flour
½ cup pecans

Filling #1:
1 small carton whipping cream
1 8-oz. pkg cream cheese
1 cup powdered sugar

Filling #2:
2 3-oz. pkgs of chocolate pudding
 (not instant)
3 cups milk
1 teaspoon vanilla
1 small carton of whipping cream

Combine crust and press into an 8 x 13" pan; bake 20 minutes at 375°F. Blend filling #1 and spread on cooled crust; mix and cook filling #2; cool. Spread on filling #1; top with whipped cream. Refrigerate for 6 hours or more. Serves 15-20.

Joan Flaherty   *Orosi High School, Orosi*

Pineapple Delight Dessert

1 6-oz. vanilla pudding mix (not instant)
8 oz. cream cheese
1 pkg yellow cake mix

20 oz. crushed pineapple
9-oz. carton Cool Whip

Make pudding according to package instructions. While pudding is hot, break cream cheese into pudding. Mix until smooth. Cover and cool. Prepare and bake cake according to package instructions. While hot, pierce cake with a fork all over the top about 1" apart. Spread pineapple (with juice) over the top of the cake. Spread cream cheese mixture over pineapple. Refrigerate to set. Top with Cool Whip. Cut into squares to serve. Serves 12.

"Quite easy and very delicious!"
Sharon Kleven   *San Gabriel High School, San Gabriel*

Pistaschio Nut Dessert

1 cup margarine, melted
1 cup flour
2 teaspoons sugar
2 teaspoons walnuts, chopped
4 oz. cream cheese

⅓ cup powdered sugar
3 oz. Cool Whip
1 small pkg. pistaschio instant pudding
1 ½ cup milk
chopped walnuts

Mix and pat into a pie pan: margarine, flour, sugar and walnuts. Bake 375°F 12-15 minutes. Cool. Beat cheese and powdered sugar until smooth. Fold in Cool Whip and spread over top of crust. Reserve half of Cool Whip. Make pudding according to package directions and pour over cheese mixture. Spread rest of Cool Whip over top and sprinkle with walnuts. Chill. Serves 6.

"Can be doubled and placed in an oblong pan and cut into squares."
Jeanette Gehrke   *Serrano High School, Phelan*

Peach Custard

3 cups flour
1 cup margarine
1 teaspoon salt
4 lbs. canned peaches

1 cup brown sugar
1 teaspoon cinnamon
2 eggs
1 large can evaporated milk

Mix flour, margarine and salt; press into a 9 x 13" buttered pan. Drain canned peaches, saving 1 cup of the syrup. Arrange peaches on crust. Sprinkle with brown sugar and cinnamon. Bake 20 minutes at 375°. Mix syrup and slightly beaten eggs with milk. Pour over peach mixture. Bake an additional 20 minutes. Serves 16.

Patricia Wolfe (Retired)   *Lakewood High School, Lakewood*

Millionaire's Delight!

½ cup margarine
3 tablespoons sugar
1 cup flour
½ cup chopped pecans
8 oz. cream cheese
1 cup powdered sugar

4 oz. Cool Whip
1 small pkg. vanilla instant pudding
1 small pkg. chocolate instant pudding
3 ½ cups milk
1 large Cool Whip
1 milk chocolate bar

Mix margarine, sugar, flour and pecans. Spread on greased and floured 9 x 13" pan. Bake 350° for 15 minutes. Cool. Combine cream cheese, powdered sugar + 4 oz Cool Whip. Spread over crust, chill. Combine puddings and milk. Beat until thick. Spread over cream cheese layer and chill 1 hour. Spread large Cool Whip on top. Grate chocolate bar on Cool Whip and serve or refrigerate. Serves 15-20.

Diedre Simon   *Norwalk High School, Norwalk*

Caramel Custard

1 ½ cups sugar
1 quart milk, scalded
½ teaspoon salt

7 eggs
1 teaspoon vanilla

Slowly heat sugar in iron skillet until sugar is brown and melted. Pour slowly into scalded milk. Add salt. Beat eggs lightly in large bowl. Slowly add hot milk and caramelized sugar to beaten eggs. Add vanilla and pour into a well-buttered dish. Place dish in pan of hot water. Bake at 325° for 1 hour, or until brown and inserted knife comes out clean. Serves 6-8.

Phyllis Kaylor   *Einstein Junior High School, San Diego*

Chocolate Mint Soufflé

20 chocolate-covered mints
  (Cortina or Schraff's, approx. 2 boxes)
1 cup chocolate chips
⅓ cup sugar

3 eggs
1 cup milk
½ pint (1 cup) whipping cream

Place mints, chocolate chips, sugar and eggs in blender. Scald milk; add to blender. Mix until smooth. Chill 30 to 40 minutes or until it begins to set. Whip cream and fold into above mixture. Pour into a soufflé dish or individual dessert cups. Chill. To serve, top with a small dollop of whipped cream and ½ mint pattie. Serves 8.

Barbara Parks   **Clovis West High School, Fresno**

Blueberry Delight

1 oblong Angel food cake
1 can blueberry pie filling
  (cherry pie filling may be substituted)

1 large pkg. instant vanilla pudding
1 ½ cups milk
1 cup sour cream

Cut the cake into thin slices. Using ½ the cake, line the bottom of an 8 x 8" square pan. Prepare pudding with the milk. Fold in the sour cream. Spread ½ of the pudding mixture on the cake. Spread ½ of the pie filling of the pudding. Repeat the layers ending with the pie filling. Chill 4-5 hours.

"A marvelous 'quickie' dessert that can be assembled ahead of time. Everyone always asks for the recipe!"

Kathleen DeBelius   **Mt. View High School, El Monte**

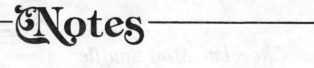

Notes

Quick Breads

Yule Logs

3 eggs
1-lb. can pumpkin (plain)
¾ cup oil
½ cup water
2 ½ cups flour
2 ¼ cups sugar

1 ½ teaspoon baking soda
1 ¼ teaspoon salt
¾ teaspoon nutmeg
¾ teaspoon cinnamon
1 cup yellow raisins
½ cup chopped walnuts

Beat together eggs, pumpkin, oil and water. Then add flour, sugar, baking soda, salt, nutmeg, cinnamon, raisins and walnuts. Pour the batter into three buttered one pound coffee cans and place in oven standing up. Bake at 350° oven for 1 hour and 15 minutes. Cool the cakes, turn them on their sides and frost with: Beat until smooth and creamy: 8 oz. cream cheese, 6 tablespoons butter, 2 teaspoons vanilla and 1 box confectioner's sugar.

"The three little yule logs can be sprinkled with chopped nuts or place tiny Christmas wreaths or sprigs of plastic holly and sprinkle with red and green decorator sugar. They can be frozen."
Liz Douglas   **Newton Junior High School, Hacienda Heights**

Apple-Cherry Bread

6 tablespoons butter or margarine
⅔ cups sugar
2 eggs
1 teaspoon grated lemon peel
1 cup applesauce
2 tablespoons milk

2 cups sifted all-purpose flour
1 teaspoon baking powder
½ teaspoon soda
½ teaspoon salt
½ cup chopped walnuts
¼ cup chopped maraschino cherries

Cream butter and sugar till fluffy. Add eggs, one at a time, beating after each addition. Add the grated lemon peel. Combine applesauce and milk. Stir together flour, baking powder, soda and salt; add alternately with applesauce mixture to creamed mixture. Stir in walnuts and cherries. Pour into a greased 8 ½ x 4 ½ x 2 ¾″ loaf dish. Bake in moderate oven 350°F for about 55 minues or until done. Remove bread from pan and cool thoroughly. Makes 1 loaf.
Mary Lash   **Paramount High School, Paramount**

Zucchini Bread

3 eggs
1 cup oil
2 cups sugar
2 cups grated zucchni (leave skin on)
1 tablespoon cinnamon
2 cups flour

¼ teaspoon baking powder
2 teaspoons baking soda
1 teaspoon salt
1 tablespoon vanilla
Optional — 1 cup chopped nuts
            or raisins, or both

Beat eggs till fluffy. Add oil, sugar and zucchini. Beat well. Sift dry ingredients together; add to egg mixture. Mix well; add vanilla, nuts and raisins. Bake at 350° in a greased and floured pan for 1 hour. Serve with soft cream cheese spread. Makes 2 loaves.
Cheré Brown   **Maricopa High School, Maricopa**

Pumpkin Bread

To Make Two Large Loaves:

3 ½ cups flour	1 cup vegetable oil
2 teaspoons soda	4 eggs
2 teaspoons cinnamon	⅔ cup water
2 teaspoons nutmeg	2 cans pumpkin
1 ½ teaspoons salt	(canned or fresh-cooked)
3 cups sugar	nuts (optional)

To Make Six Large Loaves:

10 ½ cups flour	3 cups vegetable oil
6 teaspoons soda	12 eggs
6 teaspoons cinnamon	2 cups water
6 teaspoons nutmeg	6 cups pumpkin
4 ½ teaspoons salt	(canned or fresh-cooked)
9 cups sugar	nuts (optional)

Blend together and set aside all dry ingredients. Combine and beat well the sugar, oil, eggs, water and pumpkin. Add flour mixture and beat together. Add nuts if desired.

Bake at 325° for 1 ¼ to 1 ½ hours or until a toothpick comes out clean when inserted in the middle of the bread.

This recipe can be made in a smaller loaf pans or in muffin tins if desired. Be sure to adjust the baking time for smaller quantities.

This recipe freezes well and when baked in muffin tins makes a nice addition to a school lunch.

To Bake A Fresh Pumpkin:

Cut the pumpkin in half. Place both sides, cut side down, on a baking sheet. Place baking sheet in a 325° oven for an hour or more (depending on size). Test for doneness by inserting a fork. When fork goes in easily it is done. Cool. Scrape out seeds and strings from center. Scoop out pumpkin meat and use in recipes according to directions.

Myra Lehmann   *Earl Warren Junior High School, Solana Beach*

Fresh Apple Coffee Cake

1 cup flour	¼ cup salad oil
½ teaspoon salt	1 cup sugar
1 teaspoon baking soda	1 teaspoon cinnamon
2 cups cored, peeled and	¼ teaspoon nutmeg
diced sweet apples	nuts (optional)
1 egg	

Sift flour, salt and soda together. Set aside. Place apples in medium sized bowl. Break egg over apples. Add oil, sugar, cinnamon, nutmeg and nuts (if adding). Blend thoroughly. Stir dry mixture into apple mixture just until flour is moist (mixture will seem dry). Spread in greased 8″ square baking pan. Bake 40-45 minutes. Serves 6.

Barbara Skiles   *Santanna High School, Santee*

Apple Raisin Bread

3 cups flour
2 ½ cups sugar
1 ¼ cups oil
4 eggs, beaten
1 tablespoon plus 1 teaspoon vanilla
2 teaspoons cinnamon
1 ½ teaspoon salt

1 ½ teaspoon baking soda
1 teaspoon ground cloves
1 ½ teaspoon baking powder
3 cups chopped, unpeeled apples
⅔ cups raisins
½ cup chopped nuts

Preheat oven to 325°.

Lightly grease bottoms of 2 baking pans (9 x 5 x 3). Beat all ingredients except apples, raisins and nuts, on low speed, scraping bowl constantly for 1 minute. Beat on medium speed 1 minute. Stir in apples, raisins and nuts. Pour into pans. Bake until wooden toothpick inserted in center comes out clean, about 1 hour. Cool 10 minutes. Remove from pans. Store in refrigerator.

"Freezes very well and also can be made into muffins. Take out of freezer, and heat them in the microwave for a quick breakfast bread."
Glenda Sammelman   **South Hills High School, Covina**

Banana Nut Bread

1 cup sugar
½ cup shortening
2 eggs
1 tablespoon cold water
½ teaspoon vanilla
¼ teaspoon almond extract

3 ripe bananas
1 teaspoon baking soda
2 cups flour
1 teaspoon cinnamon
½ teaspoon nutmeg
½ cup walnuts

Cream sugar and shortening. Beat eggs well; add water, vanilla and almond extract to eggs; add egg mixture to sugar-shortening mixture. Add 3 mashed bananas. Sift dry ingredients together. Add small amounts, stirring with each addition. Add nuts.

Turn into well-greased loaf pan. Bake at 325° for one hour. Makes 1 loaf.
Patricia N. Jones   **Norwalk High School, Norwalk**

Orange Streusel Coffee Cake

Cake:
2 cups flour
1 teaspoon salt
½ cup sugar
2 teaspoons baking powder
1 teaspoon grated orange rind
1 egg, slightly beaten
½ cup milk
½ cup orange juice
⅓ cup corn oil

Streusel topping:
¼ cup flour
½ cup brown sugar
2 tablespoons butter or margarine

Heat oven to 375°F. Grease a 10" pie pan or two 8" pie tins. Sift first four ingredients into bowl. Add orange rind. Make a well and add remaining ingredients. Stir only enough to dampen flour (batter should be lumpy.) Turn into prepared pans. Sprinkle with streusel topping. Bake 35 minutes or until brown. Makes 6-8 servings.

Streusel topping: Mix flour and brown sugar in a bowl. Cut in 2 tablespoons butter or margarine until consistency of corn meal.

"Quick and easy."
Pat Rice Prideaux   *Rolling Hills High School, Rolling Hills Estates*

Mr. Jones's Apple Cake

1 cup oil
1 ½ cup sugar
2 eggs
2 cups sifted flour
1 teaspoon cinnamon

1 teaspoon salt
1 teaspoon baking soda
4 cups of fresh sliced apples
1 cup nuts (optional)

Preheat oven to 325°F. Grease and flour 2 large loaf pans (9 ⅝" x 5 ½" x 2 ¾").

Combine oil, sugar, eggs in a large bowl. Sift flour and add cinnamon, salt and baking soda and add to the above mixture. Mix with electric mixer until all ingredients are blended together. Add sliced apples and mix well. Batter will be very heavy and stiff. Pour mixture into the two prepared loaf pans. Test with a toothpick to see if apple cake is done. Let cake cool in pan for 20 minutes then remove to platter or wrap in foil.

"The art teacher at our school gave the Home Economics Department this recipe. It's great!"
Jennifer Gierman   *Ball Jr. High School, Anaheim*

Our Family Fruit Cake

1 ½ lb. dates, pitted and chopped
1 lb. candied pineapple
1 lb. candied cherries
2 cups flour, sifted
2 teaspoons baking powder

½ teaspoon salt
4 eggs
1 cup sugar
2 lbs. pecan halves

Preheat oven to 275°F. Use 2 pans, 9 x 5 x 3" (or 5-6 very small loaf pans). Cut heavy brown paper to fit the bottom of the pans. Oil the pans and the papers.

Combine dates, pineapple and cherries. Sift flour, baking powder and salt together and then sift into the fruit. Mix so fruit is coated. Beat eggs until lemony, adding sugar. Mix with the fruit. Add pecans. Mix well. Pack tightly into pans. Bake 1 ½ hours at 275°F. Remove from oven and let stand 5 minutes. Brush lightly with corn syrup. Keep in a cool place.

"Makes a lovely Christmas gift."
Betty Patterson   *Lakewood High School, Lakewood*

Banana Fruitcake

2 eggs
⅔ cup packed brown sugar
½ cup cooking oil
1 teaspoon grated orange peel
½ cup orange juice
¾ cup mashed ripe bananas
  (about 2 medium)
1 cup (4 ounces) chopped, pitted dates
1 cup chopped nuts

2 cups (11-ounce pkg) chopped,
  mixed dried fruits
1 ½ cups unsifted all-purpose flour
1 teaspoon cinnamon
½ teaspoon baking powder
½ teaspoon soda
½ teaspoon salt
½ teaspoon nutmeg
¼ teaspoon allspice

Beat eggs until frothy. Beat in brown sugar and oil. Blend in orange peel, orange juice and bananas. Stir in remaining ingredients until just moistened. Pour into 10-cup fluted bundt-type dish (greased). Microwave 10 minutes on Simmer (S), 5 minutes on High or 12-13 minutes on High or until no longer doughy, rotating dish 2 or 3 times. Cool 10 minutes. Invert onto serving plate.

Cakes can be cooked in two 8 x 4-inch loaf dishes by using a lower power setting. Line bottom of dishes with waxed paper. Spread evenly in dishes. Microwave with ⅔ power 20 minutes and microwave full power 3 to 5 minutes, rotating.

To store, keep in refrigerator in Tupperware container. It will last about 2 to 3 weeks if refrigerated. Other dried fruits such as raisins, apricots, etc. may by used instead of fruit mentioned above. Serves 16-20.
Sue Nall   *Temple City High School, Temple City*

Fruit Cakes

1 lb. butter
1 lb. sugar
1 tablespoon chocolate
1 glass grape jelly (8-10 oz.)
1 dozen eggs, beaten
1 lb. flour
1 tablespoon cinnamon

1 tablespoon nutmeg
1 tablespoon cloves
1 ½ lb. walnuts
½ lb. almonds
3 ½ lb. fruit cake mix
2 ½ lb. raisins
2 ½ lb. dates

Cream the butter and sugar. Add the chocolate and jelly; mix. Add the beaten eggs and mix. Add flour and spices and mix. Add remaining dry ingredients. Mix.

Measure out 17 oz. into each tin. Decorate with candied fruits. Place jelly oll pan of water in bottom of oven. Bake at 350°F for 1 to 1 ½ hours. Cover with glaze if desired, and leave in oven which has been turned off.

"Recipe we've used for our annual fruit cake sale for 13 years."
Amber Bradley   *El Capitan High School, Lakeside*

Crumb-Topped Coffee Cake

1 ½ cups sifted all-purpose flour
2 ½ teaspoons baking powder
½ teaspoon salt
1 egg
½ cup sugar
⅓ cup margarine, melted
½ cup milk
1 teaspoon vanilla extract

Topping:
½ cup sugar
¼ cup flour
¼ cup butter
1 teaspoon cinnamon

Preheat oven to 375°F. Grease an 8 x 8″ pan. Sift flour with baking powder and salt; set aside. In medium bowl, with rotary beater, beat egg until frothy; then beat in sugar and margarine until well combined. Add milk and vanilla. With a wooden spoon, beat in flour mixture until well combined. Pour into prepared pan. Sprinkle with TOPPING (sugar combined with flour, butter and cinnamon in small bowl). Bake at 375°F for 25-30 mintues. Cut into 9 pieces.

Karin Crow   *San Diego High School, San Diego*

Raspberry-Cream Cheese Coffee Cake

1 3-oz. pkg cream cheese
4 tablespoons butter
2 cups Bisquick
⅓ cup milk
½ cup raspberry preserves
   (or boysenberry, strawberry)

Icing:
1 cup confectioner's sugar, *sifted*
1 to 2 tablespoons milk
½ teaspoon vanilla

Cut cream cheese and butter into Bisquick till crumbly with pastry blender. Blend in the ⅓ cup milk with wooden spoon. Turn onto floured surface. Knead 8 to 10 strokes. Roll dough on wax paper to a 12″ x 9″ rectangle. Turn onto greased baking sheet or cookie sheet; remove wax paper. Spread preserves down center of dough. Make 2 ½ inch cuts at 1-inch intervals on long sides. Fold strips over filling. Bake in 425°F oven for 12-15 minutes.

Make icing by combining sugar, milk and vanilla. Drizzle on top of coffee cake.

"Only use preserves for this recipe — jelly won't work! Canned pie filling may be substituted for the preserves."
Jennifer Gierman   *Ball Jr. High School, Anaheim*

Date Bread

2 cups all-purpose flour
½ cup brown sugar, packed
2 teaspoons baking powder
1 teaspoon salt
2 tablespoons butter, melted

1 egg
1 cup milk
½ teaspoon vanilla
¾ cup chopped dates
½ cup chopped nuts

Preheat oven to 350°F. Grease an 8 ½" x 4 ½" loaf pan. Sift together dry ingredients. Melt butter and cool slightly. Beat egg until light and fluffy; add milk, and vanilla to egg and beat well. Add melted butter to egg mixture. Beat the liquid ingredients into the dry ingredients until well mixed. Fold in chopped dates and nutmeats.

Place dough in greased pan and bake 40-45 minutes. Cool on rack; wrap tightly. Bread slices better if wrapped in foil and refrigerated about 12 hours. Makes 1 loaf.

Maxine S. Shepherd   *Moreno Valley High School, Sunnymead*

Banana Poppy-Seed Muffins

2 ripe bananas	2 ½ teaspoons poppy seeds
1 egg	1 ½ cups flour
½ cup sugar	2 teaspoons baking powder
¼ cup vegetable oil	½ teaspoon salt
½ cup milk	¼ teaspoon baking soda

Preheat oven to 400°F. Fill 12 cupcake tins with paper liners. Mash bananas and set aside. In a large bowl mix the egg, sugar, and oil together. Add milk, poppy seeds, and bananas. Sift together flour, baking powder, salt and baking soda. Add flour mixture all at once to the liquid mixture. Using a wooden spoon, stir just until dry ingredients are moistened. Fill cupcake liners until they are half full. Bake 20 minutes or until toothpick comes out clean. Makes 12 muffins.

Joanne Fial   *East Middle School, Downey*

Drop Doughnuts

24 ounces cooking oil	**Topping (optional):**
1 cup Bisquick	3 tablespoons sugar
3 tablespoons sugar	2 teaspoons cinnamon
2 tablespoons milk	brown bag
1 egg	

Heat oil in skillet over medium-low heat. Combine Bisquick and sugar. Stir in milk and egg. Drop by well-rounded teaspoons into hot oil. Brown on both sides. Drain on paper towels (save oil). Topping: Combine sugar and cinnamon in bag. Shake to mix. Shake cooled doughnuts in bag.

Terri Pratt   *Sage School, Palmdale*

Ricotta Pancakes

1 cup (½ pound) ricotta cheese
3 eggs
2 tablespoons salad oil
¼ cup flour

2 teaspoons sugar
¼ teaspoon salt
2 cups fresh or frozen raspberries

Combine in a blender: ricotta cheese, eggs, salad oil, flour, sugar and salt. Cover and process until smooth; push ingredients from sides of blender with a rubber spatula. Pour batter in about 3" rounds on a lightly greased griddle or large frying pan over medium-low heat. Turn cakes when bubbles form on the surface. When browned lightly on second side remove from pan. Keep warm until all are cooked. (To make ahead, cool pancakes on wire racks. To reheat, place in a single layer on a baking sheet. Cover and bake for 5 minutes in a 375°F oven). Serve cakes hot and accompany with raspberries. Serves 5.

Lianne Bennett   *Macy Intermediate School, Monterey Park*

German Pancakes

1 cup milk
6 eggs
¼ teaspoon salt

1 cup flour
6 tablespoons butter
*Buttermilk Sauce (recipe below)

With blender or rotary beater combine milk, eggs, salt and flour.

In a 9" x 13" glass baking dish, melt butter in a 400° oven until slightly sizzling.

Pour batter into the hot dish of butter slowly and bake immediately at 400°F for 25 to 30 minutes. Serve immediately topped with fruit, fruit yogurt, powdered sugar, fried apples, whipped cream, syrup, or Buttermilk sauce.* Serves 6-8.

*Buttermilk Sauce
1 cup sugar
2 tablespoons cornstarch

1 cup buttermilk
½ cup butter
1 teaspoon vanilla

In a saucepan, combine sugar and cornstarch. Add the buttermilk, butter and the vanilla. Bring to a rolling boil. Boil one minute. Serve warm over German Pancakes.

Patsy L. Jones   *DeAnza Middle School, Ventura*

Notes

Notes

Notes

Notes

Notes

Notes

Notes

Notes

Notes

Notes

Notes

Index

Lime Delight, 64
Milk Chocolate Ice Cream, 66
Old-Fashioned Chocolate Ice Cream, 66
Peach Cream Torte, 68
Raspberry Macaroon Freeze, 63
Strawberry Fluff, 66
Val's Pineapple Walnut Dessert, 62
Very Quick and Easy Ice Cream, 67

Fruits and Gelatins
Apple Crisp, 78
Banana Split Dessert, 76
Bananas Foster, 73
Blueberry, Apple or Cherry Squares, 79
Cherry Dessert, 77
Cherry Torte, 75
Choco-Bar Fondue, 72
Chocolate Fondue, 84
Chocolate Mint Delight, 73
Citronfromage (Lemon Fluff), 81
Coeurs 'a la Creme', 75
Cold Daiquiri Souffle, 74
Fried Apple Slices, 84
Fruit Cobbler, 78
Fruit Delight, 77
Fruit Fluff, 81
Fruit Kabobs with Sunshine Dip, 72
Jello Chiffon, 77
Jello Delight, 83
Lemon Fluff, 84
Lime Delight, 83
Lisa's Cherry Treats, 77
Mexican Banana Casserole, 80
Mrs. "B's", 79
Orange Cooler, 83
Peach Cobbler, 84
Peaches and Cream, 76
Pears au Chocolat, 73
Pink Flamingo, 81
Raspberry Jello Delight, 82
Red Raspberry Russian Cream, 79
Rhonda's Almond Jello, 82
Rhubarb Crunch, 78
Sprinkle Dessert, 80
Strawberry Yummo, 82

Sunshine Salad, 76
Wild Raspberry Dessert, 80
Winnie's Texas Peach Cobbler, 74
Yogurt Snow, 83
24 Hour Salad, 72

Meringues
Baked Alaska, 86
Brownie a la Alaska, 89
Lemon Angel Torte, 87
Meringue Shells, 86
Pavlova, 90
Pineapple Meringue Cake, 89
Red-Letter Day Torte, 87
Sandra's Meringue Delight, 88
Swedish Meringue Torte, 88

Pies and Pastries
Almond Tarts, 106
Apple Crumb Pie, 94
Apple Pie and Crust, 92
Bishop's Chocolate Pie, 106
Black Bottom Pie, 104
Black Russian Pie, 105
Brownie Bottom Chantilly Pie, 94
Butter Crunch Ice Cream Pie, 100
Chess Pie, 92
Chocolate Armaretto Pie, 104
Chocolate Charlotte Pie, 105
Chocolate Cheese Pie, 103
Chocolate Pecan Pie, 98
Coconut Pie, 96
Cool Chocolate Cream Pie, 99
Easy Grasshopper Pie, 103
Eggnog Chiffon Pie, 108
Florida Pie, 99
Fresh Strawberry Pie, 97
Fudge Chiffon Pie, 106
Fudge Pie, 101
Ice Cream Chocolate Pie, 93
Lemon Cloud, 97
Lemon Refrigerator Pie, 100
Luscious Lemon Pie, 95
Maple Nut Pizza, 107
Margarita Pie, 101
Mom's Cream-O-Peach Pie, 97
Mud Pie, 99
Naked Apple Pie, 97

Puddings and Custards

Quick Breads

ALPHABETIZED CONTRIBUTORS LIST

AAA

Adams, Peggy, 44, 107
Paramount HS

Alston, R.P., 7
Hosler JHS

Alt, Clyle, 55
Bell Gardens HS

Amelotte, Pam, 62
Ocean View HS

Armstead, Claudia J., 101
Jefferson JHS

Armstrong, Lois, 46, 75
Sonora HS

Artz, Sally Jean, 26, 112
Santa Fe Middle School

BBB

Baczynski, Kathie, 68, 113
Mt. Carmel HS

Baker, Roberta, 19, 87
Fontana HS

Bartlett, Clara, 76, 108
John W. North HS

Baskin-Robbins Ice Cream, 58, 59
Glendale, California

Bass, Alcyone, 84, 93
Hamilton JHS

Battu, Constance M., 7
Meller JHS

Bechok, Priscilla, 51
Bell Gardens HS

Bennett, Lianne, 35, 129
Macy Intermediate School

Bergner, Marcy, 76, 115
Kearny HS

Betz, Judith C., 65
Greenfield JHS

Blue, Karen, 80
Roosevelt JHS

Boldi, Mary, 28
Vernon JHS

Boyd, Linda, 6, 29
Claremont HS

Bradley, Amber, 60, 126
El Capitan HS

Brooks, Jane, 61
Calabasas HS

Brown, Cheré, 99, 122
Maricopa Unified HS

Bruns, Jeanne, 15
The Pillsbury Company
Minneapolis, Minnesota

Bryant, Nancy, 64, 106
Buena Park HS

Bugh, Jo Anne, 30, 109
Rialto JHS

Burkhart, Nanci, 16, 89
Hueneme HS

Burns, Jeannie, 20
Los Osos JHS

Byrum, Nancy, 21, 34
Patrick Henry HS

CCC

Chandler, Mildred, 84
Joe Walker JHS

Christensen, Libby, 35, 42
Bernardo Yorba JHS

Clark, Ann, 33, 86
Pt. Loma HS

Cochran, Myra, 22, 100
Yuba City HS

Conant, Mary, 34, 98
Grandview School

Cosart, Betty, 69, 114
Monache HS

Crider, Erma Jean, 65, 93
Sanger HS

Crow, Karen, 127
San Diego HS

Crum, Carolyn, 54, 115
Newhart School

DDD

Dalzell, Dianne, 26, 27
Bakersfield, HS

Daudistel, Kathleen, 17, 67
Hanford HS

Dauphin, Sheila, 62, 72
John Glen HS